Bread out of Stone

Books by Dionne Brand

Prose

Rivers Have Sources, Trees Have Roots (1986)
No Burden to Carry: Narratives of Black Working
    Women in Ontario (1991)

Fiction

Sans Souci and Other Stories (1988)

Poetry

'Fore Day Morning (1978)
Earth Magic (1979)
Primitive Offensive (1983)
Winter Epigrams and Epigrams to Ernesto Cardena
    in Defense of Claudia (1983)
Chronicles of the Hostile Sun (1984)
No Language Is Neutral (1990)

Bread
out
of
Stone

**recollections sex
recognitions race
dreaming politics**

DIONNE
BRAND

 Coach House Press

Coach House Press
50 Prince Arthur Avenue, Suite 107
Toronto, Canada M5R 1B5

FIRST EDITION
1 3 5 7 9 8 6 4 2
Published in Canada 1994
Published in the United States 1995
Printed in Canada

Published with the assistance of the Canada Council, the Ontario
Arts Council, the Department of Canadian Heritage and the Ontario
Publishing Centre.

Canadian Cataloguing in Publication Data
Brand, Dionne, 1953-
Bread out of Stone
ISBN 0-88910-492-1
I. Title.
PS8553.R275B7 1994   C814'.54   C94-931752-7
PR9199.3.B73B7 1994

For Zakiya and Faith Eileen

Contents

Bread
out
of
Stone

I am writing this in Cuba. Playas del Este. It is
January. The weather is humid. In Toronto I live in
the semi-detached, old new-immigrant houses,
where Italians, Chinese, Blacks, Koreans, South
Asians and Portuguese make a rough peace, and the
Hummingbird Grocery stands next to the Bargain
Harold's, the Italian cheese shop, the Portuguese
chicken place and the Eritrean fast-food restaurant.
There's a hit-and-run game of police and drug deal-
ers in my part of the city, from Christie Pits, gaping
wide and strewn with syringes, to Lansdowne and
Bloor, where my cousin and so many young men
and women walk, hustle, dry-eyed, haunted, hungry and busily, toward a fix. Here, the police carry
out this country's legacy of racial violence in two
killings of Black men and one shooting of a young
Black woman in this city that calls its racism subtle,

and the air stinks with the sanguine pronounce-
ments of Canadian civility: 'Oh no, we're not like the
United States,' be grateful for the not-as-bad racism
here. I'm writing this just after the massacre of fourteen women in Montreal and the apologias of 'mad-
man', 'aberration', in a country where most violent
deaths of women are the result of male violence.
Don't talk about the skeletons! Helen Betty Osborne
dying in The Pas seventeen years ago, tortured and
murdered by this country's fine young white men
and denied justice by this country's white law and
white law enforcers in this country with its pathological hate for Native people. What with all that, it
ain't easy. So I began writing this essay weeks ago in
Toronto but could not find the right way of starting.
Somewhere in all of that there wasn't time. The real
was more pressing than any rendering.

On the Playas del Este, near Guanabo, I'm editing
oral histories of older Black women in Ontario. The
book will become a film, but that's much later. By
now it's going on three years and I ask myself why I
started this at all. Something about recovering history, history important only to me and women like me,
so I couldn't just drop it, no matter how long it took.
And then, I remember a white woman asking me
how did I decide which to be—Black or woman—
and when. As if she didn't have to decide which to
be, white or woman, and when. As if there were a
moment I wasn't a woman and a moment I wasn't

Black, as if there were a moment she wasn't white. She asks me this because she sees her sex and takes her race as normal. On the Playas del Este, near Guanabo, I bend closely to edit the oral histories of older Black women as I remember this encounter. I put the sun outside at the back of my head.

On the Playas del Este, from Marazul to Guanabo, men yell at me and my partner, *'Aye que rica!' 'Aye mamita, cosita!' 'Que te la chupo!'* They whistle without relief. In the first days, we yell back English obscenities, shake fists at them. But they are unrelenting. And women do not own enough obscenities to fill the air. Men own this language. We ignore the gauntlet of sucking lips and stares. They do it so religiously, we realise it is a duty.

Outside the Brunswick Tavern on Bloor Street one night, a bunch of young white boys from the suburbs follow three of us. They say some words loudly, nothing understandable, but loudly and at us. They hit their feet against the pavement, come close to us. We cross the road. All of us are older than these teenagers escaped from Mississauga, but they make us cross the road. White and male, they own it.

A policeman tells a friend of mine, 'Well, obviously the guy finds you attractive. You're an attractive woman, after all.' This about the man living opposite who has hassled her since she moved into the neighbourhood. The whole neighbourhood knows he yells and screams alone in his apartment

about 'bitches' and 'whores'. They've heard him. But
the policeman sees nothing amiss with the world
here, only an occasion for solidarity with the man
living opposite who wants to kill a woman.

In my hotel on the Playas del Este, as I read about
a Black woman's childhood on the Prairies—'... and
because I was a girl I did everything ...'—I remember one noon in hilly St. Georges. I'm walking up
that fatal hill in the hot sun. This is before those days
when everything caved in. My legs hurt, I'm wondering what I'm doing here in Grenada with the sun
so hot and the hill so hard to climb. Passing me
going up and down are people going to lunch, kids
yelling to each other, the dark cooler interiors of the
shops and stores. The electricity has broken down. I
decide to have a beer at Rudolph's. The customers,
men alone or women accompanied by men, turn to
look at me. I ignore this as I've been doing walking
through town. I'm used to masculinity. It's more
colourful on some street corners; in this bar it's less
ostentatious but more powerful. A turn of the head
is sufficient. I take a swig of my beer. I open my
diary. I'm here because I've decided that writing is
not enough. Black liberation needs more than that.
How, I ask myself, can writing help in the revolution? You need your bare hands for this. I drink my
beer over my open diary and face this dilemma. I
wish I were a farmer. I could then at least grow food.
I have a job as an information officer. I write reports,

descriptions of farmers, so they can get money to produce food, from people in Europe and North America who read and love descriptions of farmers. I take the last swig of my beer, feeling its mixture with the noon heat make me cool. There's another difficulty: writer, information officer, or farmer, I will walk the streets, paved or unpaved, as a woman.

An interviewer on the CBC asks me: 'Isn't it a burden to have to write about being Black?' What else would I write about? What would be more important? Since these things are inseparable, and since I do not wish to be separated from them, I take on the responsibility of defending them. I have a choice in this.

Outside Wilson's, between Shaw and Ossington, before it closed down, Black men stare me down the street, informing me silently that they can and want to control the terms under which I appear, on the street, the sidewalk, the high wire, the string for Black women to trip on, even more vulnerable to white men and Black men because Black women cannot, won't, throw Black men to white men. I stare the brothers back. They see my sex. My race is only a deed to their ownership. Their eyes do not move.

If some of this finds its way into some piece of fiction, a line of poetry, an image on a screen, no wonder. On the Playas del Este, I am editing an oral history of older Black women, furiously.

I'm working on a film. It is a film about women in

my community. I've dreamt this film as a book, dreamt it as a face, dreamt it at a window. I am editing it on the Playas del Este: a woman's face, old and a little tired, deep brown and black, creased with everything that can be lived, and calm, a woman's face that will fade if I do not dream it, write it, put it in a film. I write it, try to make everyone else dream it, too; if they dream it, they will know something more, love this woman's face, this woman I will become, this woman they will become. I will sacrifice something for this dream: safety. To dream about a woman, even an old woman, is dangerous; to dream about a Black woman, even an old Black woman, is dangerous even in a Black dream, an old dream, a Black woman's dream, even in a dream where you are the dreamer. Even in a Black dream, where I, too, am a dreamer, a lesbian is suspect; a woman is suspect even to other women, especially if she dreams of women.

I am working on a film. Another woman is working with me. She is a friend, I've known her for eighteen years. For four of those years, I've been a lesbian, and we've lost touch. She's told me nothing has changed, people still love me even though ... I tell her everything has changed ... She tells me I've changed since ... In secret, she says I hate men and children, that's why I only want to write about, to work around, women ... She thinks my love for women must be predicated on a hatred of men and, curiously, children.

We make a warm and respectful film. She hates it, thinking it is infected by my love for women. The night of the first showing, Black women's faces move toward us, smiling. They hug us, their eyes watery from that well, centuries-old but this time joyful, thanking us for making this film.

On the shoot, we are an all-woman crew. We are three Black women and three white. I am the only lesbian. I prepare my questions, sit next to the lens of the camera, look into these old women's eyes, try in ten-minute episodes to spin the thread between those eyes and mine, taut or liquid, to sew a patch of black, rich with moment and things never talked about in public: Black womanhood. We are all nervous, the Black women nervous at what we will hear; some part of us knows that in the moment of telling we will be as betrayed as much as we will be free. I feel the other two behind me; they are nervous, too. Am I a sister? Will I be sister to their, our, silence? All three of us know that each question I ask must account for our race. I know that each question I ask must account for our sex. In the end I am abandoned to that question because women are taught to abandon each other to the suffering of their sex, most of all Black women who have the hard white world in front of us so much that the tyranny of sex is a small price, or so we think. The white women are nervous, hidden under the technical functions they have to perform. They, too, may not be able to bear the sound of this truth woven between those old eyes and mine.

Each night I go to my room alone after the shoot. More and more I skip dinner as the talk around the table flickers as a fire on the edge of a blowing skirt. It's that talk of women suddenly finding themselves alone with each other, inadvertently.

If men brag when they're together, women deny. They make sure there is no sign of themselves, they assure each other of their love for men, they lie to each other, they tell stories about their erasure, they compete to erase themselves, they rap each other in weary repetitions, they stop each other from talking. The talk becomes thin, the language grinds down to brittle domesticity. To prove that they are good women the conversations singe the borders of lesbian hate ('... well, why do they have to flaunt it?'), play at the burned edges, firing them to the one point of unity between Black and white women: fear, contempt for women who love women. I rise and leave. One night I see the fire lighting and I speak. The next night I take dinner in my room.

And the old women doing the telling, making the film—impatience crosses the other Black woman's face as they tell it. Perhaps she is not listening, perhaps she is thinking of her own life, perhaps she is going over in her mind a pained phone call to another city. But balancing on this thread, if she looks, is

something that says we do not need to leave ourselves stranded, we can be whole, and these old
women need us to do something different, that is
why they're telling us this story. This story is not an
object of art, they did not live some huge mistake,
they are not old and cute and useless, they're showing us the art of something, it is not perfect, and they
know it. They do not want us to repeat it.

I am working on a film. Another Black woman is
working with me. We're making a film about
women. Old women. All have lived for more than
sixty years, and there are five minutes in which to
speak, to feel those years. In a film, in a Black dream,
will it be all right if five old women speak
for five minutes? Black women are so familiar with
erasure, it is so much the cloth against the skin, that
this is a real question. In a Black dream, do women
tell stories? If a Black woman tells the story in a
Black dream, is it still a Black dream? The voices of
old women never frighten me. I will pay for this
fearlessness.

I listen to an old man's voice describing an old
woman's life. The other woman is now the question-
er; she has turned to the old man and asked the old
man about the old woman's life. From the back of
the room where we are filming, I suddenly ask the
old woman, 'How was it for you?' I wanted to hear
her voice. She was standing silently. We had come to
film her. My voice breaks the room, her voice

answers me, she comes alive, we rejoin the thread. The roll of film runs out. The assistant camera secures that self-doubt in a can marked 'exposed film' and loads the camera again. The old woman speaks this time.

'How was it for you?' A simple question about a dream at the window. They say it is because I am lesbian that I've asked, and that because I am a lesbian I am not a Black woman, and because I've asked I'm not Black, and because I do not erase myself I am not a Black woman, and because I do not think that Black women can wait for freedom either, I am not ... and because I do not dream myself ten paces behind, and because I do not dream a male dream but a Black dream where a woman tells the story, they say I'm not ... How was it for you? In the Black gauze of our history how was it for you? Your face might appear if I ask this. I would ask you this whatever the price. I am not afraid of your voice. How was it for you?

I've worked in my community for eighteen years, licking envelopes, postering lamp posts, carrying placards, teaching children, counselling women, organizing meetings (though I never cooked food), chanting on the megaphone (though I never made a speech), calling down racists, calling down the State, writing about our lives so we'd have something more to read than the bullshit in the mainstream press. I've even run off to join the revolution. But I haven't bent my back to a Black man, and I have loved Black women.

In the cutting room of the film someone decides that my race should be cut from me for these last sins. For each frame of film a year of my committed struggle is forfeited. My placard … my protest chant … my face on a demonstration … silent … forgotten, my poems … I am losing my life just to hear old women talk. Someone decides that my sex should be cut into me. Not the first sex, not the second sex. The 'third sex'. Only the first two can be impartial, only the first two make no decision based on their sex. The third sex is all sex, no reason. In the cutting room I reason, talk, persuade, cajole, finally insist away any erasure of these women. But erasure is their life. Yes, but it is not the truth.

In the oral histories and in the film, the women say, 'This day I did this, this day I did that, this day I did day's work, this day I took care of things, and well, we got along all right, you know. The Depression wasn't so bad for us, we were used to the hard times. But I worked just like a man, oh yes.'

As the cutting ends, I feel the full rain of hate for lesbians; it hits the ground, its natural place. It mixes with the soil ready with hate of women, the contempt for women that women, too, eat. For me, it pushes up a hoary blossom sheltered in race. I will smell this blossom, I know, for many years to come.

And it will push up everywhere and sometimes it

will smother me. I am a woman, Black and lesbian; the evidence of this is inescapable and interesting.

At a screening of the film about old Black women, a Black man first commends the film, through barely open teeth, then he suggests more detail in future films, details about husbands, he says, details about children. He wants these details to set his picture right; he cannot see these women without himself. Even now as they are old he will not give them the right of the aged to speak, to speak about what they know; he must edit them with his presence, the presence of husbands to make them wives, children to make them mothers. His picture is incomplete without their subordination. The blossom between his teeth, as it bursts into words, is not just for me.

The night of the first showing, fifteen hundred people come to see the film. The theatre crackles with joy; they recognize themselves.

You can see a hanging bridge through my hotel window on the Playas del Este. The Boca Ciega River, running underneath to the ocean, is shallow in the afternoon, deep in the evening. I only mention this because from my window on my street in Toronto the movement of the world is not as simple or perceptible, but more frightening.

Once a Czech émigré writer, now very popular in the 'free world', looked me dead in my Black eyes and explained the meaning of jazz to me.

The Atlantic, yawning blue out of my window on

the Playas del Este and beyond the bridge, pulls my eyes away from the oral histories and into its own memory. I am a little girl growing beside the same ocean on the other island some years before. I remember seeing women and men sitting quietly in the still midday heat of that town of my childhood, saying, 'Something must happen, something bound to come.' They were waiting, after waiting for crop and pay, after waiting for cousin and auntie, after waiting for patience and grace, they were waiting for god.

Exasperated after hours of my crying for sweet water, opening her mouth wide, my mama would say to me, 'Look inside! Aaah! You see anything in here? You want me to make bread out of stone?'

At a poetry reading on Spadina, another male writer tells me, 'You write very well, but stay away from the politics.' I look at this big white man from another planet and smile the dissembling and dangerous smile of my foremothers.

In my mama's mouth, I saw the struggle for small things.

Listen, I am a Black woman whose ancestors were brought to a new world laying tightly packed in ships. Fifteen million of them survived the voyage, five million of them women; millions among them died, were killed, committed suicide in the Middle Passage.

When I come back to Toronto from the Playas del

Este, I will pass a flashing neon sign hanging over the Gardiner Expressway. 'Lloyds Bank', it will say. Lloyds, as in Lloyds of London. They got their bullish start insuring slave cargo.

At an exhibition at the Royal Ontario Museum in June 1990, there is a display of the colonists' view of the plunder of Africa. 'Superior' Europeans and 'primitive' Africans abound, missionaries and marauders bring 'civilisation' 'into the heart of Africa'. 'Into the Heart of Africa.' The name of the ROM exhibition itself is drenched in racism, the finest, most skilful racism yet developed: the naming of things, the writing of history, the creation of cultural consent. Outside the museum, African-Canadians demonstrate against the exhibition every Saturday. Ten men and women have been beaten, strip-searched, arrested by the Toronto police and bonded not to come within one thousand feet of the museum. An injunction by what the demonstrators call the 'Racist Ontario Museum' prevents any demonstration within fifty yards of the building.

Still pounding the pavement for the ground on which to stand, after so long. All Black people here have a memory, whether they know it or not, whether they like it or not, whether they remember it or not, and in that memory are such words as land, sea, whip, work, rape, coffle, sing, sweat, release, days ... without ... this ... pain ... coming ... We know ... have a sense ... hold a look in our eyes ...

about it ... have to fight every day for our humanity ... redeem it every day.

And I live that memory as a woman. Coming home from the Playas del Este, hugging the edited oral histories, there is always something more to be written, something more important. You are always ahead of yourself. There is always something that must be remembered, something that cannot be forgotten, something that must be weighed. There is always something more, whether we say these things today or tomorrow, or whether silence is a better tactic.

There is never room, though there is always risk. There is never the room that white writers have in never speaking for their whole race, yet in speaking the most secret and cowardly language of normalcy and affirmation, speaking for the whole race. There is only writing that is significant, honest, necessary—making bread out of stone—so that stone becomes pliant under the hands.

There is an unburdening, uncovering the most vulnerable parts of ourselves, uncovering beauty, possibility. Coming home from the Playas del Este ...

This
Body
for
Itself

Here I listen to writer after writer talk about their work. I have plans to talk myself on 'Poetry and Politics'. It is the First Caribbean Women Writers Conference, held at Wellesley College in Massachusetts. It is probably not even necessary to say 'poetry and politics' as if those words are distinct, but I've become so used to explaining and explaining their dependency on each other to Canadian reviewers and audiences that I've forgotten that it is unnecessary here. One thing you do not have to do at a Caribbean writers' conference or perhaps any writers' conference outside Canada is explain that writers mean to change the world. But I've been in Canada so long I forget and always have to change my plans once I get out in the world. But that later. I'm in my sin. Some of the women I've read, some of the women I've learnt from, are here and all the style and gesture of the Caribbean is here, or at least what writers store up living in London and The Hague and Philadelphia and Port-of-Spain and New York and Edinburgh and Toronto. The hands flying when we talk, the drama in the voice leaking out across a metropolitan street. The language is a feast. All those cities have inflected the Trinidadian and the Jamaican and the Belizean and the Grenadian as much as they inflect each other as they meet. I've never been to Jamaica, but as I've learnt it in Toronto it inflects my speech, and I can tell if you're from Mandeville or Kingston, and here, too, I learned to tell if you're from Roseau or Marigot in Dominica or if your French is Haitian or St. Lucian. All that and the sway and gait, swing and stalk, the parry and retreat of the body. All of that is here, too. And then the sense of valour. Look how many roads each of us have footed. Who would have thought through the bush at Guaya, the red earth at Trelawny, the black sand at Mahaut, the river beds in tributaries of the Orinoco, the rice fields at Demerara that we would dust and dry our feet off here, and the leaf and sand and mud and dirt of those places would tumble out of the pages into these concrete rooms when we opened the books we write?

For several days I listen for the footfalls and they come walking hard labour and worries, they come tinkling the few pennies, the facefuls of grief, the hand-hipped sighs, the brace of steady foreheads.

For several days I listen and listen, and then it is my turn and then it comes to me and then I know what I have not heard, what has not been said. Then I know what the eyes have not read passing over that earth and river and swamp and dust, more accurately, what the eyes demur, what is missing: the sexual body. How often have I sat in a room and not heard it and not said it, myself so busy outlining the failure and the make-do, the forbearance. So busy holding the front line against certain assault, so busy knowing that it would be useless to try to express this body without somebody or other taking it over, inventing it for themselves, so busy finding it uncomfortable to live in this body and so busy waiting for and knowing that the world won't change. And then again it's self-preservation. In a world where Black women's bodies are so sexualized, avoiding the body as sexual is a strategy. So is writing it in the most conservative terms, striving in the text for conformity to the norm of monogamous heterosexual male gratification. Leaving pleasure to men, that's a strategy, too. I know that not talking about the sexual Black female self at all is as much an anti-colonial strategy as armed struggle. But what a trap. Often when we talk about the wonderful Black women in our lives, their valour, their emotional strength, their psychic endurance overwhelm our texts so much so that we forget that apart from learning the elegant art of survival from them, we also learn in their gestures the fine art of sensuality, the fleshy art of pleasure and desire. The women who taught us these are strewn as heavily across our landscapes as the women who taught us to struggle against hardship. Often they were and are one and the same. Didn't we take in their sweetness, their skinniness, their voluptuousness, their ample arms, their bone-sharp adroitness, their incandescent darkness; the texture of their skin, its plumminess, its pliancy; their angularity, their style when dancing, their stride across a piece of yard that sets the yard off, their shake as they sense the earth under their feet, their rock, the way they take music in their shoulder, the way they pause and then shimmy and let it roll? Didn't we take in their meaning?

Often we cannot find words that are not already taken up to say this. I had been thinking a long time about this, that we couldn't describe this with any confidence or control, and here it was two days and not a word. At Caribbean writers' conferences you do not meet with resistance on politics, just on what kind of politics. The politics of the body, the female sexual body, is closed or open only to the taken-for-granted. At another conference, I remember a male writer being nonplussed at the suggestion that Ayei Kwi Amah could be questioned about the portrayal of white women in *Why Are We So Blest?* Of course the white woman represented Europe and her torture the recovery of African manhood, he asserted, as if this symbolism was sacred and somehow inalienable. And another defended the Virginal in Jacques Roumain's *Masters of the Dew* as the correct symbolism for the pristine land ravaged by the colonisers. It is amazing to me that this symbolism in this context escapes being criticised as hackneyed, dated and simplistic. And so if this language belongs only to male writers as the most radical inscription of colonialism/anti-colonialism, then how does any one else dare use it, even those of us whom the body belongs to, how do we loosen it from this 'high moral' use which of course also charges it with its opposite?

'Poetry and Politics' became less pressing then, as I sat listening to everyone avoid the body for itself, and even more redundant because if we couldn't have our bodies we couldn't have anything. So when it was my turn, I apologised for bringing sex up and said these things and read my story, 'Madame Alaird's Breasts', about how girls in an all-girls school love the French mistress's breasts. Laughter. And I warned against the laughter because laughter is another strategy. But I read in spite of where I knew this story was going and might be swamped, in the only way that people know how to read the female body, because if I did not make room for this story ...

Outrage. I hear that some think that I've ridiculed the woman in the story. I've been indecorous. No one tells me directly, but I sense that I've crossed the line. Only the feminists and the lesbians talk to me after that. I'm late and I hear that the next session is charged with questions about lesbianism and homosexuality. It has taken the lunch hour for the story to sneak up on the audience. The lesbian *double entendre* has just dawned on some. After lunch some astute man rises to challenge, as if the conference has to put this thing back in its place, these girls loving a woman's breasts. Michelle Cliff, the novelist, presenting in the next session, has to answer for my indiscretion. I've fired the lunch tables and the low-lighted theatre with indignation. When I come near, people stop talking; friends look glazed, as if they do not want to show me the least recognition lest they be associated with my travesty, or they whisper behind my back. I retreat to the hotel, hurt by the reaction, and I know I've called it upon myself. I was uncomfortable with the seamless, undifferentiated female sex constructed in the talk, the sex without sexuality for herself, and I was bothered that this woman might be me or my aunt or my mother or my grandmother and part of her might be missing, part of her she might enjoy for herself. I was worried that she might not want to be a symbol for any writer's pain, mine included. I was sure there were times when she did not want to be our mother or our role model for forbearance, times that she wanted to collapse under the weight of our dependence and the tyranny of our description.

To write this body for itself feels like grappling for it, like trying to take it away from some force. Reaction to the story confirms this territorial pull and tug. One never sets out to be unloved. I could return to the fold by saying that it was an innocuous story not meant to sheer the seamlessness, not meant to offend and not meant to have fun just so, by itself. In my room I examine loneliness until Joan Riley's girl-child comes looking for someone to talk with. I take her back to her room. I'm not sure if Joan feels the same as everyone else. I cautiously tell her how I feel. She says, 'Don't worry about it. You have to write the truth and it doesn't matter if nobody likes it.' Then she tells me the outrage in the community, in London, that met her book, *The Unbelonging*. We talk late.

I have to trust what I know. I write in one of my stories that my grandfather put the sound in my name and my grandmother put the silence after it. It was a silence rich and profound in its comment about how my grandfather came at the world. It was a silence that grew even more textured as their life together continued and she ceased to speak with him entirely. Instead, she sent messages to him from one part of the room to the other through us, her grandchildren, even though she was only two feet away. 'Tell you grandfather I said. ...' He at first tried to respond directly, but she answered with more messages. 'Tell you papa I can't hear him.' Then he understood and he sent messages too. After their long life together, what she meant and what he understood I can only surmise. He understood that she meant that he could say nothing more that could change her world. My grandmother had made a departure. I once wrote of her 'swimming in the brutish rain/ at once she lost her voice/ since all of its words contained her downfall/ she gargled instead the coarse water from her eyes/ the incessant nights/ the crickets call/ and the drooping tree,/ breathed, in gasps what was left in the air/ after husband and two generations of children.'

But where my grandmother left my grandfather to silence, she revealed to us the grand and dark elegance of language in stories that filled our nights without electricity, our nights of dry faces and often empty stomachs. Using her stories like food, she filled us up with legends of flying women who inhabited the billowing darkness. As if letting out the day, rearranging the world, she in her nightly cadences would set the events, the real meanings of the world, right. The blunt edges of the days, the brutality of want, she would set to their dialectic, their causes and their redemption. Every child where I was born heard these stories but what I remember about her stories of the soucouyant and la jablesse, women so unlike her, is how they drove her voice to its most guttural and its most honeyed.

Through these sounds she had sent messages for us, her woman-children, parables on how we should live in the world. She could not think herself past her time and her context, so her statements though profound were somewhat unfinished. They only hinted at the real. Her body huddled in a question mark on the bed most days. She was, however, as suggestive as she could be about taking power, her fingers thick with wash water. But her warnings were sprinkled frequently and sufficiently enough to be libation for the woman-spirit in us: her chuckle at a soucouyant changing her skin in a barrel of rain water, the smiling suggestion that she was a shapely woman once.

I think that women learn about sexual pleasure from women. The strict code of heterosexuality would have us think that we come upon sexual pleasure when we notice men or that we should. But codes are only necessary where there is variation, questions of power. The need to regulate reveals the possible. Despite all this, I think we catch a glimpse, we apprehend a gesture. We remember despite the conditioning we receive as women not to remember other women, or to be ashamed of that memory or to think it immature. This gesture is where we learn our sexuality, however—lesbian and straight. When I try to trace my lesbian sensibility I arrive at early images: the woman living up the street from me, nicknamed 'Sours' for a red and sweet candy; the woman who lived across the street, whose laugh rippled seductively up and down our street; the woman caught in the last sunlight of High Street, San Fernando, smiling a gold-toothed smile; one aunt of mine hidden in the dawn on the verandah, surprising another sneaking in by singing her the calypso 'Where you been last night, Caroline' and chuckling. These were signals of sensuality, desire and pleasure, these and more have become part of my consciousness, as much in the historical landscape as the woman getting up at dawn, hoe over her shoulder, leaving the slave barracks for the field.

Janice Lee Liddell in an essay in *Out of the Kumbla* writes, 'The image of mother—giver and nurturer of life; teacher and instiller of values and mores—has indeed become one of the most persistent of Caribbean archetypes. In the Caribbean as in nearly every place in the world, any criticism of this most celebrated and procreative human role will more than likely be met with wild-eyed contempt by women and men, both of whom have so internalised the myths of motherhood as to ignore its harsh realities. ... It has been difficult for women—and practically impossible for men—to admit that this most honorable woman-destiny can be and usually is both restrictive and debilitating; that society's pressure to be "the good mumma" almost always obstructs more creative opportunities than it provides.'[1]

In male writers' work like that of Jacques Roumain or Earl Lovelace or George Lamming the female body is either motherly or virgin, which amounts to the same thing—like land to be traversed or owned. Their descriptions are idylls, paeans, imaginary, and inescapably about territory, continent. Here Lovelace, speaking through his female narrator Eva in *The Wine of Astonishment*: 'And here is this girl, Eulalie Clifford from River Road, belle of the village, a young filly frisking her tail, moving with that smooth, soft teasing womanness, with her eyes bold and down-looking and smiling and though her dress make out of the same material they use to make dresses for any girl, Eulalie Clifford dress have a kind of spring in it, a kinda thing, a life in it that when she walk, her skirt hit her hips and the cloth dance up and hold onto her body and strain against her flesh as if is not cloth at all but a living thing. Here is a girl ... swinging across the unpave roads, watering the mouths of every male that she see and making the old women smile and nod their heads and want to reach out and touch her with their hands to bless.' [2] The female is made for a man, carnally knowledgeable in the essential female body but young, hapless, inexperienced, waiting for inevitable control and ownership. Here Jacques Roumain in *Masters of the Dew*. Here it is the woman as country, virginal, unspoiled land, as territory for anti-colonial struggle. These are not writers with bad intentions, but their approach to the Black female body is as redeemer of the violated, and builder of the binary pedestal.

In female writers there is the safety of the mother, the auntie, and protection from and resistance to the outside. In *Crick Crack Monkey*, Merle Hodge's women figures dominate the novel as much as they dominate the interiors of their own lives. Though women do not dominate political life or life outside the home they control what they can, given the social alignment of women and men in Caribbean society. Not usually found in nuclear patrilineal families, they run their families through matrilineal structures. Tee, the narrator, is growing up with her Tanti after her mother has died in childbirth and her father has sailed to England. Tanti is a joyous struggle of a woman prone to laughter, drinking and fierce defence of her children and her class. Her children are Tee, Toddan (Tee's brother) and Mikey (their teenage cousin). None of them are Tanti's birth children but they are no less her children. Aunt Beatrice, Tee's mother's sister and known in Tanti's lexicon and the lexicon of Tanti's street and household as 'the bitch', wants to take Tee and Toddan from Tanti's life, a life which Beatrice calls 'niggaryness'. Tee ends up going to live with Aunt Beatrice and by the end of the novel is on her way to England, ambivalent about Tanti's world, which she has been made to feel ashamed of. Yet Tanti's world is the place where she has felt most safe and most human, a refuge from the embarrassment and rejection she encounters at Aunt Beatrice's. *Crick Crack* is a genteel treatment of the growing up of a girl in Caribbean society; the themes of race and colonialism are consistent with male texts, but Hodge's novel draws from inside the lives of women. That heroic and all-powerful grandmother or aunt becomes the source of the most lyrical descriptive writing. Tee sees her grandmother Ma in the description. 'Ma awoke every morning with a groan quickly routed by a brief loud cheups. She rose at a nameless hour and in my half sleep I saw a mountain shaking off mist in one mighty shudder and the mist falling away in little drops of clouds. The cheups with which Ma greeted the day expressed her essential attitude before the whole of existence—what yuh mus' beat-up yuself for? In the face of the distasteful and unavoidable, the unexpected and irreversible, all that Ma could not crush or confound with a barked word or surmount with her lioness strength, she reacted to with a cheups, more or less loud, more or less long.' [3] We get a sense of Tee's physical, sensual and historic connection to Ma: '... the agreeableness of sitting clamped between Ma's knees having one's hair plaited. The cream air in the middle part of the day was like time staring at itself in a mirror, the two faces locked dreamily in an eternal gaze. I was Ma's own-own bold face Tee, harden' as the Devil's shit but that is yu great great grandmother, that is she, t'ank Gord. Sometimes when the others were not about she would accost me suddenly: "An who is Ma sugar-cake?"' [4]

I was curious about what drew such howls of rage in Joan Riley's works and understood when I read them, finding not the heroic mother or auntie or grandmother but the exposed, betrayed, valiant and violated female self, the vulnerable and fearful, the woman waiting for the probable invasion. But what must have damned Riley was her pointing to the men as the source of this exploitation in those women's lives. The novel *The Unbelonging* is about a young girl, Hyacinthe, who is sent to England to meet her father, leaving her Aunt Joyce and two friends, Florence and Cynthia. She is eleven on arrival in England and encounters a brutal father and a stepmother who is spiteful in the face of her own battering by the father. Living in coldness and poverty in one of England's Black slums, Jamaica, Aunt Joyce, Florence and Cynthia become more and more Edenic in Hyacinthe's dreams. Riley intercuts the texts with Hyacinthe's dreams, which are filled with such longing and fear that the young girl suffers from bed-wetting at the waking to reality. Her father beats her every day until the day that her period arrives and then he begins to threaten her sexually. Hyacinthe's life is one of terror of her father's beatings, of his sexual assaults and of the racial assaults she also confronts daily in the schoolyard and classrooms. Her character moulds into self-hatred, fear around her race and her sex. Not only does she not belong to England and white people, she does not belong to her body, her growing womanness. Her female self is a dangerous thing she is forced to carry around; it is the symbol for attack for the men she encounters as she flees her father's house and is put in care until the age of eighteen. As much as her Black self is the signal for attack to a white British world, in the world of white people and Black men, Hyacinthe walks a tenuous and despairing line, her self-revulsion and isolation tightening around her daily. Even the dreams that are idyllic at the beginning of the novel become more and more suffused with the terror of the present and the possibility that the dreams are not true.

The burden of the body is as persistent an image in Caribbean women's literature as it is in Black women's lives and only becomes less so in the aged woman who has already passed through—like Aunt Joyce's body: 'They had been lucky to get a place to the front and she pressed closer to Aunt Joyce's reassuring bulk as the crowd surged against her.' [5] The progress of Aunt Joyce's body over the course of the novel from 'big and impatient ... good natured face' to 'a withered old woman ... the lined drawn face, with its sunken eyes and air of death,' is directly linked to Hyacinthe's sanity. She returns to Jamaica to recover herself, depending on the safety of Aunt Joyce's bulk and her own anticipation of passing into that safety. Instead she meets an Aunt Joyce as emaciated and timorous as herself and as horrifying. 'And inside her deep down, buried inside her woman's body, trapped and bleeding in the deepest recesses of her a young girl screamed.' [6] Riley leaves us with an image of the Black woman still to be healed, made whole between the mother and the damaged, a Black female self 'trapped and bleeding'. Riley's book had violated the law of silence set down for Black womanhood. She had said that far from being there for the sensuality of men or the ravaging like land by the colonist, it was injured and recoverable only by itself, if at all.

In *The Unbelonging* the gaze of race and the gaze of sex are almost identically described: 'She hated the communal showers, hated having to step naked and defenceless along its length, her blackness exposed for all to see, to snigger about behind her back. She knew they did it, though they were always careful to hide it from her.' [7] 'She had managed to put the whole incident aside, when he started to watch her bathe. Hyacinthe hated these times. She would sit in the water dying from embarrassment. "Wash yourself girl" he would say and she would hang her head in shame, as she scrubbed the top part of her body, praying that he would leave before she had to stand up. Many times he would order her to stand up and wash and the knowledge of the lump in his trousers would force her to obey. She hated her body, felt shame at the wisps of black hair that had started to grow on her pubic area and the fact that her breasts had started to swell.' [8] 'You must watch your father' her stepmother tells her when she begins to menstruate. 'You old enough for him to trouble you like he did with your cousin.' 'They don't like neaga here' her father tells her about the whites. The warnings are the same, sex or race.

In another of Riley's novels, *Waiting in the Twilight*, the heroine, Adella, ends up living in a 'yard' with other women in her predicament— unmarried, children, poor and dependent. The 'yard' in Jamaican city life is an enclosure of shanties and rooms populated primarily by women and children. In the yard Adella learns early of the precariousness of dependence on men. The yard is the terrain of hunger, male exploitation, make-do, economic dependence and bitterness. Women are not only hardened by but blamed for their fecundity, even as it is their duty to breed, to become the mother. Old age is the only time that women escape the precarious and dangerous load of fecundity. Until then, and if they survive womanhood, a litany of hardship is allotted to their sex and race. It is impossible to find in Riley's novels Black women experiencing sexual pleasure. From the beginning of the novel *Waiting in the Twilight*, the female body is portrayed as burdensome, useless, out of the control of the self. The 'threat' of fecundity overshadows the lives of the women in the novel. The woman as mother, as fallen woman once she has children out of wedlock, and as rejected woman because she cannot produce a son defines Adella's life and the lives of the Black women on the London streets where she lives.

After we've read *Waiting in the Twilight* we wonder why these women are alive at all; if this despairing picture of Black womanhood that Riley paints is correct, what possible reason would Black women have to live? 'Pain neva kill nobody,' Adella says. Pose Riley's description of the female life against the passage quoted earlier from Lovelace's *Wine of Astonishment*. The collusion in female objectification by the old women is embedded in Lovelace's gloss, as is his complete romanticization of Black female life, but Riley shows this collusion as a cruel sentence passed on from generation to generation. We cannot dispute the sobering similarity to real life in Riley's novels though she gives no relief from its dreadfulness. Some woman some time, I think, must have had some agency in the sensual, in the pleasurable and the sovereign.

Jamaica Kincaid's work is distinct for its challenge to these themes on Black Caribbean women's bodies. She examines the sensual connections between mother and daughter in a revealing and candid way in *Annie John* and in a way which before her intervention only male Caribbean *Bildungsroman* held sway. Reading the anti-colonial text as gendered,

she posits the mother as body text for the growth of
Annie even as the mother assumes her own physical
integrity. In the chapter called 'The Circling Hand',
Annie observes the mother having sex with her
father and feels betrayed and revolted. In the mother's distance from Annie in this act, Kincaid allows
each sovereignty even as this sovereignty separates
the two. Kincaid is also not afraid to have her char-
acters claim the lesbian erotic as a feature of female
life. Annie's fascination with the lawless, the free,
through an intensely sensual relationship with 'the
red girl', breaks with the tradition of not disclosing
the range of the erotic that women experience and
defies the danger of disclosing any eroticism which
is not for male consumption. But it would seem as if
no Caribbean woman writer can resist the great big
mother, whether she is a grandmother, auntie or
elder.

In Kincaid's collection *At the Bottom of the River*, in
a story called 'My Mother', the spectre of the mother is grand and beautifully terrifying: 'My mother
removed her clothes and covered thoroughly her
skin with a thick gold-coloured oil, which had
recently been rendered in a hot pan from the livers of
reptiles with pouched throats. ... She uncoiled her
hair from her head and then removed her hair alto-
gether. Taking her head into her palms, she flattened
it so that her eyes which were by now ablaze, sat on
top of her head. ... Then making two lines on the

soles of each foot, she divided her feet into cross-roads. Silently, she had instructed me to follow her example.' [9] And perhaps no Caribbean woman writer can resist the knowledge that the mother is her own future. Here again Kincaid is expressing all our fear, entitlement, ambiguity and self-recognition. 'My mother has grown to an enormous height. I have grown to an enormous height also, but my mother's height is three times mine. Sometimes I cannot see from her breasts on up, so lost is she in the atmosphere. One day, seeing her sitting on the seashore, her hand reaching out in the deep to caress the belly of a striped fish as he swam through a place where seas met, I glowed red with anger ... I adorned the face of each moon with expressions I had seen on my mother's face. All the expressions favoured me.' [10] This is a mother to rival Paule Marshall's Silla in *Brown Girl, Brown Stones* in power and physicality. In Kincaid's next work of fiction, *Lucy*, the mother is further away but present. To create herself anew, the protagonist stops reading her mother's letters.

Both *Annie John* and *Lucy* are anti-colonial and anti-patriarchy texts, making critiques of both conditions simultaneously. But they also do something else. The heras break with the compelling conventions of both. The texts reject these conventions and talk about what we are really concerned with in our daily lives: not only the external, the encounter with 'whiteness', but the ongoing internality.

Kincaid contents herself not with creating paradigms but with unfixing the fixed, with going about our business.

In *Out of the Kumbla*, the Caribbean critic Carol Boyce Davies discusses the 'female self' as largely concerned with mother-daughter identity and makes only passing reference to sexuality and sensuality. Even when faced with explicit sexual and sensual references, as in the work of lesbian writers Audre Lorde and Michelle Cliff, or when referring to what I read as a lesbian-erotic passage in Kincaid's *At the Bottom of the River*, Boyce Davies submerges these in a Freudian (reversal) analysis of the mother-daughter relationship. 'Mother-daughter' is the only 'female' self Boyce-Davies allows within what she says is an examination of Caribbean women writers' 'self definition which takes into account both gender and heritage.' Though calling her focus a Black feminist critical one in her essay 'Writing Home', she ignores the 'female self' in anything other than the mother-daughter relation. These big mothers overwhelming our texts cannot fit so neatly into Euroconscious categories precisely because they exist despite those categories. And one wonders if this temptation to fit them in is not itself a strategy to regularize our relationships as proof of our sameness, humanness, by way of European paradigms. Or perhaps it is just a preoccupation with Christian moral rectitude—the good daughter and the good

mother. Or perhaps it is fear of sexuality itself and
the way it leaks out of these texts, defying literary or
social category.

I grew up in a society where sensuality was not
forbidden, where calypso crystallised the sexual *double entendre*, where two days of Carnival encouraged
sexual display, but this did not mean sexual freedom
for women. All the openness and display took place
within the context of serving male sexuality. Perhaps
there were more exceptions, or at least I'd like to
think so, of female sexuality for itself, but the street
corners were full of anti-female sexual heckling, and
despite the cross-dressing Carnival Mondays (mostly men dressed as women), on Ash Wednesday a lesbian could be raped for such public display.

For me the most radical strategy of the female
body for itself is the lesbian body confessing all the
desire and fascination for itself. 'Madame Alaird's
Breasts' was my first overt admission of that desire
and also an honest rendering of what really hap-
pens. We hear rumours. And of course we hear them
in the language. The earliest rumour that I can find
of lesbian life in the Caribbean comes from the late
nineteenth century. Leaving the plantations where
women's labour was paid half of men's, women
dominated the cities in number and culture. They
made up the majority of the poor and they organised
into an underclass with a style and culture which
they themselves made. In Port-of-Spain, Trinidad,

for example, there used to be gangs of women called jamettes. Jamette means loose woman. It is taken, suggests Bridgette Brereton, from the French *diametre* or underworld. The word is still current for a brash, loud, sexually 'loose' woman or whore. That women lived in various kinds of relationships, including lesbian relationships, is suggested by David Trotman in his article 'Women and Crime in Late Nineteenth Century Trinidad'.

My grandmother used to say, 'Don't go out there and behave like a little jamette,' and she used to say that my uncle was turning into a jamette man, and my aunt would throw words at her mother, saying 'You already say I is a jamette' when my grandmother disapproved of her going out.

Most notorious among the jamettes, Trotman says, were Bodicea and Petite Belle Lili. I remember hearing about Bodicea when I was a little girl, the connotation being that not only was she a whore but also a lesbian and a brawling fighting woman. Trotman suggests that indications of lesbianism can be found among the jamettes, if we look at the court records of the day which say, for example, that this or that woman and her friend were involved in a fracas, or this woman and her friend were charged with beating up a man who had bothered them. The housewifing of women in the early twentieth century, the use of the police to contain their culture and styles drove the culture underground, leaving only fragments of it in the language, the parts of it that referred to male sexuality. So jamette had become strictly whore by the time I heard it.

Zami, meaning woman-loving, or zaming and making zami meaning women fucking or making love. Sometimes the language is less obvious because it is so commonly affectionate. So my aunt says when I ask her if she ever knew any lesbians that, yes, there was a woman once, a beautiful woman, she says, who told her that she loved her and my aunt said, 'Well, you know how we talk so I never thought anything of it.' Until her husband told her what the woman really meant. But I remember the way women's names were said, suggesting brashness because these women were also fighters, well, because they had to fight.

What made me interested in these women was the insistence in the culture that they did not or don't exist and that they did not craft our sexuality and therefore our history. Perhaps they do not appear because they are inconvenient, as inconvenient as Tanti is for Aunt Beatrice in *Crick Crack Monkey*. In the construction of neo-colonial classes through gender and privilege, such sexual leakages are inconvenient, unseemly; they do not conform to the structures for complete control and exploitation of women within these classes.

There is a curiously 'civilising' discourse in all this—pulling the Black female body into line.

Perhaps the great big mother appears in all our texts, bursting the seams and out of control in order to remind us.

Just
Rain,
Bacolet

Back. Here in Bacolet one night when the rain falls
and falls and falls and we swing the door wide open
and watch the rainy season arrive I think that I am
always travelling back. When the chacalaca bird
screams coarse as stones in a tin bucket, signalling
rain across this valley, when lightning strafes a blue-
black sky, when rain as thick as shale beats the xora
to arrowed red tears, when squat Julie trees kneel to
the ground with the wind and I am not afraid but
laugh and laugh and laugh I know that I am travelling back. Are you sure that this is not a hurricane?
Faith and Filo ask. 'No,' I say, with certainty, it's just
rain. I know this, it's just rain ... just rain, rain is like
this here. You can see it running toward you. And
this too, don't fight the sea and don't play with it
either, that shell blowing means there's fish in the
market and, yes, I'd forgotten the water from young

green coconuts is good for settling the stomach, you have to cut or scrape the skin off shark before you cook it, otherwise it's too oily and this prickly bush, susumba, the seed is good for fever, and the bark of that tree is poison ... Knowing is always a mixed bag of tricks and so is travelling back.

On one side of this island is the Atlantic and on the other the Caribbean Sea, and sometimes and very often if you drive up, up the sibilances of Signal Hill to a place called patience, yes, Patience Hill, you can see both. There are few places you can go to without seeing the sea or the ocean and I know the reason. It is a comfort to look at either one. If something hard is on your mind and you are deep in it, if you lift your head you will see the sea and your trouble will become irrelevant because the sea is so much bigger than you, so much more striking and magnificent, that you will feel presumptuous.

Magnificent frigate drapes the sea sky, magnificent frigate. Bird is not enough word for this ... nor is it enough for the first day just on the top of the hill at Bacolet that red could draw flamboyant against such blue and hill and cloud and the front end of the car floats between them ...

... at first I went alone, was brought, arrived, came, was carried, was there, here, the verb is such an intrusive part of speech, like travelling, suggesting all the time invasion or intention not to leave things alone, so insistent you want to have a sentence without a verb, you want to banish a verb.

Anyway, I was carried by the way they'd cut the road, fast and narrow, and with magic because always it was impossible for two cars to pass each other but it happened, and magic because one afternoon cutting through the rain forest on Parlatuvier Road to Roxborough but right in the middle of the rain forest a woman and soft in the eyes and old like water and gentle like dust and hand clasped over the hand of her granddaughter little girl appeared, walking to Roxborough. So we stopped, seeing no house nearby that she may have come from or be going to. The road was treed and bushed on all sides, epiphytes hung from the palmiste and immortelle, and we stopped to her 'Thank you, darling, thank you. What a sweet set of children! I going just down the road. Thank you, darling.' To be called darling and child, we knew it was magic because no one, no stranger in the last twenty-four years of my life and in all of Faith's living in the city we had left, had called us child and darling. We stared, grinning at her. We settled into her darling and child just like her granddaughter settled into her lap. Magic because she had appeared on the road with her own hope, a hope that willed a rain forest to send a car with some women from North America eager for her darling, her child, or perhaps she wasn't thinking of us at all but of walking to Roxborough with her granddaughter to buy sugar or rice and her darling and child were not special but ordinary, what she would say to any stranger, anyone, only we were so starved for someone to call us a name we would recognise that we loved her instantly.

One day we are standing in a windmill—no, standing in a windmill, trying to avoid the verb to meet, which is not enough for things that exist already and shadow your face like a horizon. We climbed to the top of the windmill at Courland Bay with S. The wooden banisters have been eaten away by termites. They've eaten the insides of the wood, ever existing, trying to avoid the verb to meet, as I, we. We learn that you cannot hold onto the banisters though the outside looks as it might have looked then. She had told us what year, some year in another century, 1650, or perhaps 1730. We climbed to the top, passing through the bedrooms the windmill now holds, the bats' droppings in the abandoned rooms, then outside to the top, up the iron stairs. That is when she said that the mill had been here, a sugar mill, a plantation, and there were the old buildings, traces of them, there since then. That is when she showed us the old building, near the caretaker's house, near the cow roaming on her thick chain, near the governor plum tree, tangled up in mimosa and razor grass, but not covered and not all of it there. We learn that you cannot come upon yourself so suddenly, so roughly, so matter of factly. You cannot simply go to a place, to visit friends, to pick mangoes on your way to the beach and count on that being all. You cannot meet yourself without being shaken, taken apart. You are not a tourist, you must understand. You must walk more carefully because you are always walking in ruins and because at the top of a windmill one afternoon on your way to the beach near Courland Bay you can tremble. At the top of a windmill one afternoon on your way to bathe in the sea when you stop off to pick some mangoes you might melt into your own eyes. I was there at the top of the windmill taken apart, crying for someone back then, for things which exist already and exist simply and still. Things you meet. I am afraid of breaking something coming down. Something separates us.

We leave the top of the windmill and the owner, who is still talking about carving it up and selling it in American dollars, and go to talk to the caretaker who feels more like home, more like people. He knows the kind of talk we need, talk about the rich and the poor, talk about why you can weep when looking at this place, talk that sounds quiet in the trembling and razor grass, as if he understands that there are spirits here, listening, and we must wait our turn to speak, or perhaps what they are saying is so unspeakable that our own voices cut back in the throat to quietness. This is where it happened and all we can do is weep when our turn comes, when we meet. Most likely that is the task of our generation: to look and to weep, to be taken hold of by them, to be used in our flesh to encounter their silence. All over there are sugar mills even older, filled with earth and grass. Now everything underfoot is something broken.

Faith went to the Rex last night. It was Friday, the latest Robert Redford movie was on. Not because she likes Robert Redford but because it's the only cinema and she loves the movies. She loves the Rex with its hand-painted sign, freshly painted every Wednesday when the movie changes. I am scared of the movies, scared since I was small. Scared because I was afraid of people and because the movies were new and something you had to learn to go to and to take care of yourself when you were there. Going to the cinema, you needed money and you needed to dress up and you were in public where people could see if you were dressed up or had the money. And if you didn't have enough money, you had to sit in Pit where there were a lot of rough boys who made rude remarks about girls and tried to touch you and went to the cinema just to do this and to heckle the screen or imitate the star boy if it was a western. I was fearful, too, that what I would see on the screen would confirm the place we occupied in the world. We were going to see how much better white people lived than we did and how far away the reach to that living was because we would have to reach into white skin to live it. The re-enactments always came up slightly short. The lipsticked white beauties and the slicked-back white macho twisted us into odd shapes on tropical streets, made us long for black turtle-necked sweaters, blue jeans and leather jackets and cowboy hats. So having only this memory of cinema in the Caribbean, I didn't go to the Rex with Faith to see *Indecent Proposal*, and she went because she didn't believe me, being much more adventurous than I and having grown up when film wasn't new or scary but the first primer of the culture, as much as the primary text of mine was the British canon. When she came back she said it was lovely, yes lovely, that the whole cinema heckled Robert Redford and Demi Moore and the guy from *White Men Can't Jump*. They laughed and jeered at American romanticism. Perhaps something in a Black cinema in a Third World country makes a screen full of white patriarchy and desire as money seem silly, unlikely and grotesque—unbelievable. Nobody was buying it and not just because it was a silly-ass movie in any terms but because nobody was buying the general screen. She said she finally felt a whole audience feeling like her and more—outside the screen and critical, belonging to another intellectual cosmos, one that was not craziness but sense. And nothing that ever came on the screen at the Rex would be seen with anything other than this sense. She had spent so much of her life in the lonely deconstruction of the American movie text that the

Rex was home, the true meeting of the hegemonic and the counter-hegemonic, and the counter-hegemonic made more than sense, it was normal. But deeper, they were laughing. The crowd, probably blue-jeaned and longing in every other way for America, found America laughable. So I changed my mind about the Rex, but I still never went, still so fearful that Faith went every Friday by herself or with a woman we'd met who was waiting tables in a restaurant. One Friday night I met her on the street in between a double bill. She was looking for coffee; the street that circled the harbour was packed brightly with young women and men, liming, hanging. Her face came luminous and teary in the crowd. I went to meet her. I thought that she might have been lonely because I hadn't gone with her, but it wasn't loneliness, it was ordinariness that moved her. She wanted to keep walking in the crowd on Friday night and going to the Rex.

Travelling is a constant state. You do not leave things behind or take them with you, everything is always moving; you are not the centre of your own movement, everything sticks, makes you more heavy or more light as you lurch, everything changes your direction. We were born thinking of travelling back. It is our singular preoccupation, we think of nothing else. I am convinced. We are continually uncomfortable where we are. We do not sleep easily, not without dreaming of travelling back. This must be the code written on the lining of my brain, go back, go back, like a fever, a pandemic scourging the Diaspora. Go back, the call words waiting for an answer. How complicated they can get, all the journeys to the answer, all the journeys, physical and imaginary, on airplanes, on foot, in the heart and drying on the tongue. Faith and I glimpse it here. When we first get off the airplane and slip into our skin, the gravity of racial difference disappears. But it is this and more, a knowledge we slip into, a kind of understanding of the world which will get us through. Here we only have to pay attention to what we do. One night Vi called, said, Do you want to see a leather-back turtle? She's laying her eggs on Turtle Beach. We went. I felt called as I do for every event here. Surrounded so by spirits, history, ancestors, I give over to their direction. I realise that I live differently in Canada. I live without connection to this world with its obligations, homage, significances, with how you are in the soul.

A woman told me a story last week of how a man from Quebec who had laid floors for a living had all his money stolen on the beach by thugs. 'He show me his knees from working and he knees mash up,' she said. 'And when I look at them knees I say to myself if that man ever kneel down on them knees and pray for that thief, put a light on that thief, god help him. Is so people does look for trouble.' She understood the power in his knees in ways that the man from Quebec could not. Knees like that were a weakness where he came from.

So I was called to a great thing. The leather-back turtle came up on the beach like this that night. Every May they come up on Turtle Beach to lay hundreds of eggs. I had forgotten. And when the eggs hatch after six weeks, tiny turtles scramble to the sea under the predaceous swooping of pelicans and frigates. The hotel, its light and customers, intrude on this beach, but this part of the sea is inscribed on all the generations of leather-backs, so they come even as investment and real-estate brokers gobble up the sand and water. One came making circles and digging her back fins into the sand and then she left without laying. The sand there was too hot, Vi said. So she went back into the sea waiting for another time. Later, down the beach, we came on another. When my eyes became accustomed to the dark I saw her. She was ancient, her head larger than a human's but somehow human-like and her eyes full of silver tears, her skin, black with tiny white spots, wrinkled. She dug a nest in the sand behind her, measuring, measuring with the length of her fin. Then I heard her sigh, a sound like an old woman working a field, a sound more human than human, and old, like so much life or so much trouble and needing so much rest. This is how old I'd like to be, so old I'll cry silver, sigh human. But I must say here truly how I felt, as if she was more than I or

more than human, higher on the evolutionary lad-
der, beyond all surmising or calculation, nothing
that we could experience, greater than us not
because we had said so but because she was. I
watched her for over an hour, dig and measure, dig
and measure, and then lay her eggs. I went closer to
see them and remembered eating one as a child on
another beach. 'I've seen this before,' I told Vi.
'When I was little,' eating something it had taken the
leather-back fifty or sometimes seventy years to
make, delicate and soft after more than half a century. I remembered the torch lights cutting shadow
along that other beach and my grandfather digging
for the eggs of this now-endangered species. She
was seventy by her size, broad as the span of my
arms and as tall as I lying down, and when she was
done and had sighed again she covered the hole in
the sand and began circling, camouflaging the place
she had lain her eggs, making other places looking
the same until I could not tell where she had laid
them. A leather-back turtle cries on a night like this,
her tears are silver and when she is done circling,
doing all that she can do, she heads laboriously for
the sea. She seemed tired. She spun down to the
shore, waited for a wave and then plunged, washed,
splendid, rode into the sea.

We are so eager to return, our powers of recognition isolate only the evidence in support of a place.
So I did not mention the unnecessary clutter of

tourists and cameras which had to be policed and ...
So I took this as a gift, this intimacy I intruded on at
Turtle Beach, with the tourists, the ones we had to
shush, and the lights and the hotel and the cigarette-
smoking man Vi told to 'have a little respect.' I mea-
sured only the space that the leather-back and I
occupied. I took it as part if not all the answer to
going back.

We drank Carib up to the last drinking spot on
the Northside Road to Moriah, Castara and
Parlatuvier. We stopped, asking for my grandmother's people in Moriah. She was born in Moriah to
Angelina Noray and a man named Bobb. I asked an
old, big, gentle man coming down the road where
the Norays lived, knowing that all I needed to do
was mention a last name and whether they had van-
ished or were still alive the name would conjure
them. 'Well, the ones on the hill or on the flat?' he
asked. 'I'm looking for my grandmother's people,
she leave here long, long ago. She had a brother
name Dan.' 'A long time ago. Daniel. Well, is the
ones on the flat you want then.' We looked to where
he pointed in the high lush valley that is Moriah. I
did not go to the shelf in the hill to see them, just said
thank you, comforted, and pointed the car up
Northside Road, remembering his arm pointing to
the luxuriant bamboo where my people came from.

'See, see Moriah, Moriah, Moriah. See, see
Moriah, Moriah, Moriah. Dingolay lay lay lay lay oh

...' See Moriah. This children's song comes back to us, and Vi and I speculate as to what it might have meant. We hope it was a place to escape to. We know that they do a wedding dance here, only ceremonial now, dating back to the nineteenth century, 'See, see Moriah, Moriah, Moriah. See see Moriah, Moriah Moriah Moriah. Dingolay lay lay lay lay oh dingolay one boy one girl ...' Marriages not being allowed to property, we speculate that perhaps the enslaved ran to this high valley to dance the wedding dance as a sign of revolt and self-affirmation.

Just last night in the Scarborough public library we listened to an architectural anthropologist from the University of Florida talk about the way the French built sugar mills and the way the British built sugar mills and the way the Spanish built sugar mills, how they used the wind and the water, their drains and ditches, the proximity of their great houses to the mills ... He said nothing about the people who built them and worked them because he was an architectural anthropologist and not concerned with people, but he did make an attempt to appease us by saying that the Moriah wedding was a blend of the European and the African cultures. It never occurred to him that it was in poor taste and perhaps even foolhardy to stand before us and call European conquest and African enslavement a 'blend'. It didn't occur to him to think of the Moriah wedding as a mask, a more than simple duality suggesting mockery, irony, picong, self-affirmation, absence, change, recognition and antimony. Later, he introduced his protégé, also from the University of Florida, who was a social anthropologist who said that he in fact was interested in the people who worked in the mills and that at Courland Bay he had found English crockery in a place that he had identified as slave quarters. This suggested to him that the slaves and the master had a relationship of cordiality. He would have had us believe that at Courland Bay, which used to be one of the largest slave plantations, and boasting hundreds of acres and hundreds of slaves, the master let his slaves drink in imported English teacups. He beamed in a kind of self-absolution, a kind of brotherhood, and sat down to the grateful applause of the representatives of the local and the island government and the historical society.

'That is what does happen when you let people into your business.'

Parlatuvier, Parlatuvier, Parlatuvier, old talk, old talk or furnace pipe, what is the meaning? Castara, Castara, cast away, cast away, next to Englishman's Bay. I'd rather the mystery of names, and I'll keep to myself all the women on the island and where we met them. These maps are for passing word of mouth, the way to another place like Moriah for purposes of dancing and lovemaking. And we left some conversations for lesbian anthropologists who also read looks and movement and the inclination of figures and the shortness and silence of this passage as cryptic as the signals for escape.

A long time ago I think I fled this place because flight is as strong as return; the same, often. One is not the end of the other or the beginning of the next, and often when we go back all we can think of is flight. And in flight ... But this time I wanted to stay. We wanted to stay. This ease we slip into leaves us stranded once we have to disappear again. The closer we get to home the more we disappear, contemplating immigration lines and police lines and bank lines and just bullshit lines.

'I know why we don't want to go home. What we have to deal with is not understandable, it's crude and mean-spirited.'

'We live with hatred all around us, don't we? Exploding the skin.'

'It damages us. Damages every part of us but mostly your soul.'

'We have to live so small there; here at least there is the simple, simple assumption of goodwill.'

Bathurst

Bathurst Subway. I say it like home. It's an uneasy saying, as uneasy as the blue-grey walls, rattling trains, late-laden buses and shrieking streetcars. But when I first came to this country, this city, at seventeen, it was a sign of home.

Funny how home is the first place you look for even if you are running from it, you are nevertheless always running toward it, not the same spot but a spot you're sure that you'll know. Maybe home is an uneasy place so Bathurst felt like it, not the trains or the grey walls but the people who passed through it that year, the feeling of common purpose, the intensity of new Black pride, the possibilities for justice and the joy in these. It was 1970, the Civil Rights Movement, Black Power, Black Consciousness. Martin Luther King's passivity had been repudiated; joining the system, assimilation, was out; armed struggle was a much debated possibility. The computer take-over at Sir George Williams University had awakened the Black Power movement in Canada. The new generation here, a mix of those from old families and new immigrant ones, did not respond to the subtleties of Canadian racism with the same patience and reticence as their elders had.

Bathurst Street was the centre of the Black community in Toronto. As soon as you got here, if you were an immigrant, you made the pilgrimage to Bathurst Street. Wherever they took you after the airport, whether it was an apartment on Westlodge or Palmerston or Dupont or in St. James Town, the next morning they took you to Bathurst Street. It must have been this kind of place for the Black people before the Caribbean Blacks came, too. Around Bathurst was where most of the community ended up, pushed by jobs and prejudice to where they could rent a place. I heard that only the Jewish people would rent to Blacks here in the forties and fifties, that they themselves had been pushed by jobs and prejudice to Spadina. And in the sixties, a Canadian economy hungry for cheap labour brought flocks of Black labour to Bathurst Street and its surroundings.

They first took you to Bathurst and Bloor to locate you, your place, the point from which you would meet this country. And your relationship to it was clear since this was the only oasis of Blacks in the miles and miles to be learned of in the white desert that was the city. They took you here for you to get a sense of your new identity, the re-definitions you knew were coming but could never have anticipated though you had some sense when you gave yourself up to the journey that you'd emptied a place for them. Bathurst was the site of new definitions. To a woman thirty years earlier, this is where she walked out of her maid's dress and into the hairdresser's and her day-off best dress to the Thursday night dance, the streetcar to the Palais Royale to jump the jive to Count Basie, the United Negro Improvement Association socials and raffles. This is where young women like me thirty years later walked out of the conservative, keep-quiet, talk-right, act-like-a-lady-even-though-nobody-considers-you-one, get-a-nice-job, find-a-husband, know-your-place, you-can-only-hope-for-so-much-as-a-Black-woman, pull-in-your-lips, corset-your-hips, smile, take-what-you-get dream that society laid out for us and our mothers urged on us, and walked into our naturals—no make-up, no bra, no corset, no European idea of beauty—walked into the Afroed and African no-bullshit-rhetoric beauty of ourselves.

In 1970 Bathurst Subway was filled with dashikis, African wraps, gold big-hooped earrings, Panther blue shirts, black leather jackets, Black Power fists raised in greeting and the murmur of sister this, brother that, the *salam aleikum* of the Nation of Islam.

We memorised Malcolm X's autobiography, heeding his hard lesson, and Fanon's *Wretched of the Earth* we quoted with biblical humility. We were lucky that year to have the Movement, and even if the white community around us pretended bewilderment and thought as they still do that it was all something from south of the border, we were living it, the Movement I mean, and Bathurst Subway was the passageway, the nexus from which we all radiated, the portals through which we all passed, passing from Negroes into Blacks, from passive into revolutionary. The stakes were high for us. We were never going to be able to cut our hair and join brokerage firms twenty years later, we would never be able to shake our heads and pass it all off as youth, we didn't go to Woodstock, we couldn't stand John Lennon and the Beatles, we couldn't care less if Elvis lived or died, he was just another culture-vulture to us, and though we loved Jimmy Hendricks we felt him a lost brother. Our children would never have the floating televised-out Generation-X-only-means-white-folks-angst; theirs would be a deathly desperation. There was no comfortable identity to fall back on, no suburb waiting, it wasn't our mothers and fathers we were defying, it was history. We watched hippiedom crowd our destiny with freedom off the TV screens. We said, Ain't that just like white folks. What we were leaving was hell, and we could not later boast about what fun it was or, turned conservative, how naïve we were. This was for keeps, no excuses to our children, no forgiveness from racial history.

Just outside at Bathurst and Bloor, I was one of a troop of pamphleteers steadily working this corner from 1972 to 1978. I had spent the first two years getting the hang of the city, drudging it out at several dead-end jobs and raising my consciousness in arguments, at study groups, in a Black students' organisation, at community events and partying, which ended up being the same as studying. Whatever the event, I always ended up on this corner or in the subway, waiting for a sister, waiting for a brother, waiting for a group of sisters and brothers, going to a meeting, a party, a picnic. Whatever. We seemed to like the way we looked there in full African regalia, affecting the seriousness and righteousness of our movement. It was our new station, the capital of our new country. I cannot recall any actual music playing on the corner or in the subway, but there seemed to be music, we seemed to walk to some music, and I know that we deliberately made the noise of our greetings press the spaces between the walls and move into the street. I know that our new awareness needed affirmation in public display because we were waking up from the dead. So I know there must have been music, and in those days, if you can call a mere twenty-five years ago 'those days', there were no beat-boxes so it must have been us singing a cappella, calling the *orishas* to Bathurst Subway.

Rather, summoning the *orishas* brought here since 1600. 'You say that by baptism I shall be like you: I am black and you are white, I must have my skin taken off then in order to be like you.' That very astute brother, Olivier Le Jeune, whose real name nobody remembers, dissed the Jesuit missionary Paul Le Jeune in 1632. Now here we were in another century come to call him on Bathurst Street.

In 1972 it was busy with the traffic of the Black People's Conference, just south at Harbord Collegiate, when Imamu Amiri Baraka came to town with his entourage, and the Harambee singers opened the plenary, their a cappella filling the auditorium until the walls seemed charged with righteousness and imminent freedom. Bodyguards for Baraka lined the stage, looking terrible and exciting. In 1973 it was for the Free Angela Davis Campaign. Then I was also a dancer. I was also a writer. Well, then I thought I could do anything. So the day Fania Davis, Angela's sister, came to town to talk at Henson-Garvey Park, I was not only helping with the food but dancing with the Sans Aggra Dance Group in orange and black to the theme from *Shaft*. I'm not sure that I didn't do a poem, too. I was that frontish, as my grandmother used to say, and that energised, that committed to the struggle that I thought that I could do anything.

Bathurst Street led to College, to 355 College Street where the UNIA hall was, and there my

education began. The Sino-Soviet split drew a line
down the middle of the hall on African Liberation
Day meeting nights and 'Soviet imperialism' and
'Sino opportunism' were flung across the borders
even as the African Liberation Day celebration got
organised. The first day I walked in as a representa-
tive for the Black Education Project, not fully comprehending that my organisation was on the Soviet
side, I agreed with some proposal of the Maoists, not
fully comprehending their cunning. I got drawn up
by a veteran. Well, I had as much of a good feeling
for Mao as for Lenin. That hall is where Dudley
Laws was pushed into service as a compromise can-
didate between the old guard conservatives and the
new radicals in the community. Duds was really a
moderate with a kind and malleable heart, somebody the radicals could be frank and persuasive
with and the conservatives comfortable. So in 1994,
today, when I hear the Metropolitan Toronto Police
call him a radical it makes me want to chuckle. I can
still see Dudley's harried face trying to hold the
Black Education Project back from encroaching on
the whole hall, trying to control the unruliness at the
ALD meetings, trying to stop the disrespect for the
elders, keeping some insensitive meeting-goer from
sitting in the sacred chair Marcus Garvey sat on.
Shows you how right-wing the backlash is when a
moderate gets called a radical. That time the hall was
full of police spies; you knew them the way they

always raised the question of security for the march or rally, introducing a deadly tone in the room's otherwise eager buzz.

In 1978 we were working the four corners of the intersection just after the killing of Albert Johnson by the cops. Only months before they had killed Buddy Evans down on Spadina Avenue. And those who could have saved his life had said that he was just a nigger and left him to die. Now Albert Johnson was shot on his staircase in his house on Manchester. A Jewish sister and I were flyering the corners, she on the south-west, I on the north-east. It was for the rally to protest the killing of Albert Johnson. The rally would start on Manchester, go to Henson-Garvey Park (in 1978 some of us called Christie Pits the Henson-Garvey Park), then up Oakwood to the police station on Eglinton near Marlee. Suddenly some MLers appeared on the north-west corner, giving out another flyer about another rally on the same day. The MLers were ruthless opportunists. It didn't matter that their rally had no support from the Black community groups, it didn't matter that we were trying to bring all the groups and support groups together—they had the right line and could represent the masses of Black people better. They weren't even Black, though their new strategy was to organise groups of people of colour into 'people's' organisations. Well, we got into a shouting match on the corner, the Jewish sister and I yelling that they were deliberately misleading the people and that they must be working for the police. They, yelling that they had a right to organise their own rally and that we were Soviet pawns. We called them a distraction, accused them of trying to sabotage the rally and went back to flyering furiously. At some point I think they left. The day of the rally not a cop showed up in uniform and the police station was locked and ghostly. We wanted to break down the doors but Dudley said no. When Albert Johnson's sister sang 'By the Rivers of Babylon', water came to our eyes. We've been weeping ever since. One killing after another, one police acquittal after another.

By 1978 the African liberation wars—Angola and Mozambique—were over and the local brutalities took a hold of this corner. Now we're fighting a rearguard action against the cops and the newspapers here.

The juke box at Wong's, just up the street from the subway, I swear has the same hits playing as twenty years ago. I can still go there, punch in A73, and Aretha Franklin will sing 'Respect'. The juke box never changes and the cooking never changes; it's always good. From time to time, Mrs. Wong (I've never seen Mr. Wong) changes the plastic on the tables for new plastic or tries to redecorate in some other *cosquelle* wallpaper. It always ends up looking like Wong's, where you don't go for the decor but for the food.

The barbershops are diagonally across from the subway, and on any given day you can listen to the most fascinating and ridiculous conversations. All of the rhetorical tropes of the Diaspora are in lavish display against the designs of geometric buzzes and high fades. The barbershops and hairdressers, too, are a passageway. From Afro to gheri curl to OPH (other people's hair—no girl, this ain't nobody else's hair, I paid for it) to weaves to fades and back, back to Afros. Lesbian dreads. The new political statements get made here in the way we cut our hair and cut ourselves a bright figure against the pull of the dark suits and pale dresses the rest of the subway crowd offers. We can't stand drabness no matter what our sex.

Across and up the street, the Home Services Association is more venerable. This is where Black veterans of the wars found support and solace when racism denied them the respect they deserved; this is where the Library of Black People's Literature used to be until 1977, and today uniformed cadres of children take classes on the weekends to heal them from the weekly racism in the mainstream educational system.

The arteries of Bathurst Subway carry Black life and industry along its bus and streetcar routes up to Vaughan and St. Clair, Oakwood and Eglinton, and down to Alexandra Park. All those faces, worried, anxious, waiting, eating, approving, disapproving, hurrying, wondering where the hell the Vaughan Road bus is and what to cook for supper tonight and why is that child in those big clothes and his mother must be working damn hard to pay for that leather jacket … all of that is home for me.

The full press of Black liberation organising has ground down to a laborious crawl. We're now battered by multicultural bureaucracy, co-opted by mainstream party politics, morassed in everyday boring racism.

But just as we took over this subway, I notice other takeovers. The city is colourising beautifully. In a weird way this is a very hopeful city. When you think of all the different people living in it—the Chinese, the Italian, the Portuguese, the South Asians, the East Asians and us—you've got to wonder how all of that is happening. And you've got to be hopeful despite people. They all may not know what they're doing, and they may hate each other's guts, and Black folks know that we're on the wrong side of that shit all the time, but something's happening. People make room and people figure out how to do the day-to-day so that life's not so hard.

At this little Italian neighbourhood bakery on Hallam, I'm having a *latte macchiato* and a piece of bread with cheese. It's just after Caribana 1992 and the woman behind the counter comes out limping to sit down so we start to talk about her feet. I tell her she shouldn't wear high heels, it's not good for her;

she says she's been wearing them so long she can't wear flat shoes. I tell her get some Birkenstocks like mine, she brushes me off. Then she says, look at it this way, your people bring all this money to the city, they want the money, but when there's a little trouble you're bad people, same with us. I perk up, sensing solidarity. So we talk about Caribana and how some ordinary rowdiness gets blown into a riot because cops always want to just draw guns when they see Black folks. It's like it's in their genetic coding or something. But big business don't mind if we fill up their hotels and restaurants and clothing stores. Then she says, it's like the CHIN picnic—Johnny Lombardi is doing his best. Look how many years, such a nice picnic, now the feminists want to stop the bikini contest, what's wrong with it, eh? I didn't know that she was going there so I laughed and argued for a bit and finished my *latte macchiato*, not wanting to lose a new friend.

In a taxi with a young Sikh cab driver, I strike up a conversation about phone bills. He says his phone bill is so high because his wife is making so many phone calls home he can't take it, he's told her to stop. I tell him she's lonely, leave her alone. He laughs, he says, yes, it's true and affection for his wife washes his face. But he says he doesn't make enough and the bill will take up his whole cheque. I realise that he doesn't know that you don't have to pay it all at once, and I introduce him to the art of paying for the long-distance habit which will last his wife perhaps the next ten years. Yes, I'm still assuring him as I leave the cab, as long as you pay something they won't cut you off. It's Canada, they live on credit.

What I want to say is that this city has a life that white folks, at least the ones that run things and the ones that write letters to the editor, don't know about and can't talk about because they're too busy reading their newspaper for the latest validation of their stereotypes. But the Italian bakery carries hard-dough bread and the Korean grocery store sells ackee and hot Jamaican patties and sticks of cane.

And why can't we just assimilate, as the letters to the editors frequently demand, and why we mustn't, and why must we just hang around Bathurst Street wearing red with canary-yellow shoes and outlandish weaves, with purple and blue drop curls. We have a different sense of style. We can't tolerate the ordinary, it's too suffocating.

Not to mention that it occurs to me that white people migrated to Canada for different reasons than Black people, and there we might find the irreconcilable nature of our encounter. Not to talk, but to talk of history: by the time we hit this moment white people were flying out of their history and Black people toward theirs. It might be necessary for white Canadians to eschew their past, running from ethnic wars in Europe, ethnic hierarchies and poverty. For them the romance of making a new life without the past is compelling so the idea of a Canadian—something to be filled in ready-made with a flag and an anthem and no discernible or accountable past (despite colonisation by the British and the French)—appeals to white Europeans needing an empty space, a space without painful history, a past antiseptic and innocent. And when they met the descendants of the French and the British here, their interests would coalesce in the desire for a pristine and forgetful nation. Black people, on the other hand, living in Canada, coming to Canada, living in the United States or the Caribbean had and have the task of the necessary retrieval of our stolen history. We do not wish to run from our history but to recover it; our history is to us redemptive and restorative; in as much as it binds us in a common pain it binds us in common quest for a balm for that pain.

And what would these letter writers—the English, the French, Ukrainians, Germans, Italians, Portuguese, etc.—have in common anyway except their 'whiteness' when they disingenuously inveigh 'people who come to Canada should just become Canadians.' Well, that would take science. Not will. Say amen to Olivier Le Jeune three hundred and seventy-four years later.

So we're not going any place, and we're not melting or keeping quiet in Bathurst Subway or on Bathurst Street or any other street we take over—Eglinton,

Vaughan, Marlee. If our style bothers you, deal with it. That's just life happening, that's just us making our way home.

In 1992 Malcolm is still around. The Fly Girls and B Boys wear his X on leather and Kente caps and listen to him on Walkmans, sampled against a rap back-beat. The spiral curls and drop curls orange, purple and electric blue on eighteen year olds, the bubble dresses, the batty riders, the over-sized sweats in satin, silk and cord even as I face the generational divide are not entirely incomprehensible to me. I recognise myself.

Today the voices of incense sellers and vegetable hawkers waft over the notices of the protests against the latest police killing of a member of the Black community. It's a corner charged with the kind of keeping on that mixes luck and hope and resignation with the way things are going to be if you're Black in this city. And then again there's a whole lot of virtuosity in just getting over.

Job

It was that tiny office in the back of a building on Keele Street. I had called the morning before, looking for a job, and the man answering remarked on that strong Scottish name of my putative father and told me to come right in and the job would be mine. Yes, it was that tiny office in the back of a building on Keele when I was turning eighteen, and I dressed up in my best suit outfit with high heels and lipstick and ninety-seven pounds of trying hard desperate feminine heterosexuality, wanting to look like the man on the phone's imagination so I could get the job. When I went to that tiny office and saw the smile of the man on the phone fade and the job disappear because all of a sudden it needed experience or was just given to somebody else and, no, there would be no interview and if it were today I would have sued the pig for making me walk away with my eighteen-year-old self trying not to cry and feeling laughter, that laughter that Black people get, derisive and self-derisive rising inside my chest. Yes, it was that man on the phone, that office on Keele Street, that man's imagination for a Scottish girl he could molest as she filed papers in the cabinets in the tiny office, it was that wanting to cry in my best suit and high heels I could barely walk in and the lipstick my sister helped me to put on straight and plucked my eyebrows and made me wear foundation cream in order, I suppose, to dull the impact of my blackness so that the man in the tiny office would give me that job. What propelled my legs back to the subway was shame. That I could ever think of getting such a job, even so small and mean a job, that some white man could forget himself and at least see me as someone he could exploit, and I was willing to be considered as someone to exploit. It was 1970. A kitchen then, maybe, but not an office. My sister worked the kitchens of hospitals, and that is where I did find a job the next week, and that is where we waited out the ebb and flow of favour and need in this white place.

Cuba

I don't know if it was 1959 or 1960 when my oldest uncle, hearing about the revolution in Cuba, took a fishing boat from the south-east coast of Trinidad, from the village of Mayaro from which on a clear day you can see Venezuela, and headed for Cuba to see what was going on. I only remember hearing the story and recalling his face which would break into a golden grin, the kind of grin that had secrets and that was laughing at you as much as it laughed with you. All of his teeth weren't gold, just a few in the front, suggesting a kind of dangerous but charismatic style. I heard this story and I thought him mysterious and daring since my grandfather always said that he was a damn fool for doing it. Going to Cuba, I mean.

It might have been Mon Repos Scheme. We lived at 21 McGillvray Street, Mon Repos Scheme, San

Fernando, three houses from the bottom on the left-hand side, and when we didn't have the rent we walked from the bottom of the street rather than coming in at the top. The housing office was at the top. The rent was twelve dollars a month and we were rarely paid up. We didn't think that we were poor; we thought that we were well off, but two or three weeks of every month a penny's worth of sugar or a handful of rice begged from a neighbour was how we survived. You had to be poor to live in the Scheme, but no matter what, people made up their hierarchies of worth and there were classes within the class. The next door neighbour's husband, who never spoke, had a job with Texaco so they were better off; they built a fence and raised chickens, too. My big sister's best friend's father had a job at McEarneny Auto and they had a car, which made them a little better off though there were lots of them and their only brother had water on the brain so he sat at the window holding his head and memorising licence plates. And then everybody was suspecting everybody of having money on the quiet; in fact, everybody tried to persuade everybody else that they had money on the quiet to prove that they were a better kind of people. My family thought that we could carry this off by good decorum, so we were never allowed to go outside and play in the street nor did we go to Sunday school—the first because it would look as if we were out of control, 'a bunch of

wild niggers', and the second because we didn't
have any good clothes or good shoes or, my family
suspected, good manners, to wear to Sunday school.
That is how I never got religious. Anyway, with all
this pretending not to be poor, the street was very
quiet and circumspect except now and then came the
long robust laughter of somebody trying to be so
decent that one day a roar of indecent laughter rips
out of their chest. Being decent and well off were one
and the same, which made being poor and indecent
one and the same, too. When this laughter was heard
the houses that it didn't come from turned their
noses up and called the offenders 'indecent' until the
day that it ripped out of their throats and the tables
were turned. Sometimes people did not talk to each
other on the street just to keep a distance and to keep
indecent people in their place. And sometimes, if
some family had found religion, Seventh Day
Adventist or Church of God, they would make it
their pious duty to visit people and be condescend-
ing, as they had found another way of being decent
and of a better class of people as they were nearer to
god himself. Everybody tried to be different from
everybody else but without any true basis in fact.
Everybody there had just fled some hard country
place like Manzanilla or Moruga or Tableland or
Morne Diablo. Each of the houses had two bedrooms, a living-room, a kitchen and a bathroom. The
house had room for everyone in my family except

those who were on the outs for one reason or another —unapproved pregnancy, delinquency, quarrels. It was room for ten or eleven people at any given time and for more unfortunate relatives from the country who were in harm's way or looking for work. So much so that my nightmares are of packed rooms. But we were well off because my uncle was a teaching monitor and he was learning to be a teacher at the training college at Mausica. One morning when I was eight or nine he couldn't get to Mausica because I had stolen the twenty-five cents that he used to pay the car to take him the forty miles there. I put it in my sock, and he did not discover it even though he told us all to take off all our clothes just as we were about to leave for school. My grandmother saw me cunningly move it into my shoe and said nothing. Only that afternoon when I returned from school, sated from the richness of twenty-five-cents' worth of belly cakes and achar and great popularity, she rubbed my ears between her thumb and forefinger and whispered, 'I see what you do. Never let me see you do that again.' She kept it between us and I never forgot the shame. To tell the truth, at one point in the day I panicked, not knowing if I could spend all of the twenty-five cents and what would I do with the change.

Close to this time I heard of Cuba again. All the radios on the street were tuned to Radio Trinidad for the world service of the BBC news. Out of the doorways, as everyone played their radios high, came the voice of the imperial newsreader about Playa Giron and, not many months afterward, about the Cuban Missile Crisis. About the Bay of Pigs, my family boasted that Fidel had buried the Yankees in the sea. About the Cuban Missile Crisis, they boasted that Kennedy had faced down Khrushchev and communism. This last boast won out after days of argument about how serious and hard the Russians were and if Kennedy 'think that he was man' let him deal with Khrushchev. The discrepancies in the family positions on Playa Giron and the Missile Crisis were due to the curious Caribbean nationalism my family held and to the propaganda of the Cold War and the red menace which they were equally steeped in. Or let me not lie—they also loved America. They knew nothing about communism except for dire warnings against it and the way in which it was hauled out to discredit union leaders and anyone who seemed to be earnest or dangerous. But they nevertheless were fascinated with the idea of communism. Anyone who was serious or steadfast they called a communist. They would say, 'He is a communist, you know, so don't try nothing,' or 'You see my face? I is a communist, don't play with me,' or 'You lucky I is not a communist, you get away.'

Cuba faded in my family after that, as if it had left the planet. All that American might turned our eyes to what was important to admire and love: money,

education, progress. I didn't take Spanish at the
Naparima Girls' High School. Instead I took French,
eyes on Europe and the French teacher's breasts.
And then again we were a practical country. It made
no sense to look to Cuba. We understood who was
boss and we lay down or went along, and then again
the expulsion of Cuba from the world gave the
tradesmen and the middle-men with no imagination
a good deal of power and ascendancy in the rest of
the Caribbean. They were not misguided or pawns
as in our hearts we would have liked to believe. No
great morality play at the centre of which some
great, torn man is placed. They were just small-busi-
nessmen who knew a good swindle when they saw
one. They were just import-export middle-men with
a new gimmick: democratic government. They knew
the nationalist rhetoric, they might even have
believed it, and they were prepared to use it to get
the import franchise for small, useless commodity
items in Trinidad, like plastic dinette sets and plastic
flowers, and the big, wasteful commodity items like
motor cars for which they stopped the train from
Port-of-Spain to San Fernando, all of which would
later lead to a run on wrought-iron bars for shop
windows and house windows and shop-till-you-
drop in Miami.

These practical things might have had no signifi-
cance if not for a feeling I had of not heading for any
place worthwhile if things were going the way I was

seeing. I had seen things where I could tell what was happening and all the other children could tell, too, sometimes without anything being said. My Standard Four teacher liked her light-skinned son better than her dark-skinned son, and she was always screaming at her dark-skinned son, slapping him behind the head, and we all knew why because all the light-skinned girls sat in the front of her class-room and all the dark-skinned ones in back. Before that, at Miss Greenidge's private school around the corner when I was three or four, this light-skinned, rich people's son named Garnet was the teacher's pet. And when he lent me his slate pencil and I lost it Miss Greenidge said that I was an 'old nigger' who didn't know what to do with good people's things and whacked me with a guava switch and stood me outside for the afternoon. Colour, too, separated my big sister and me when she took me to my first day at big school. She was darker and all her friends made her cry, laughing and telling her that I was not her sister and she was lying. Well, I didn't like them making my big sister feel unhappy and worst of all wanting to disown me. These things you knew since then and you say if I have to live I wouldn't live like that. What makes people go the other way is my question. That's harder isn't it? Don't they become so sated, like I was with my poor uncle's twenty-five cents, that it isn't fun? Seeing poverty is not enough, I know, and seeing hurt.

But then again, it might have been a small skinny old man that I'd seen in the newspapers right then, a man who was a scholar and a national treasure already and who had said that he did not need a piece of paper from a university to validate his intelligence. Such a slight man and such confidence, he reminded me of my grandfather, lean as a leaf and dismissive of racial colonial trappings. His name was C.L.R. James and I liked the daring of that statement, the superiority of it and that while we were drunk in the local glamour of a Black national leader in a just-decolonising nation, he had been friends with Trotsky years before.

The just-returned Black national leader, author of *Capitalism and Slavery,* was afraid of him even though C.L.R. had been his mentor and his teacher, which I suppose might have accounted for the fear. Still, *Capitalism and Slavery* was a ground-breaking work on the growth of the so-called Western World on the back of Black slavery. I wondered at fourteen why Eric Williams would be afraid of C.L.R. James, given that Williams was a radical himself, or at least he represented the radical idea that Black people in Trinidad could throw off the yoke of colonialism and govern themselves and that British colonialism had exploited and oppressed us while telling us that we were inferior. So why with such powerful and persuasive, necessary and vindicative ideas did C.L.R. James make him fearful? Why did the architect of

Trinidadian Black nationalism fear the architect of the Pan-African Congress?

C.L.R. had not gone to Oxford and had become a Marxist intellectual revered all over the world. Williams had gone to Oxford and returned with a rhetorical style that would make a decolonising nation shake its collective head in intense admiration, rivet a nation to the radio and fill the capital's streets with masses of people chorusing his 'Massa day Done'. But C.L.R. fascinated me, even as I was glued to the radio listening to Williams' speeches in that audacious, anti-colonial, mocking staccato, that play and vaunt of language from his University of Woodford Square. Maybe it was in the names of the parties they were to lead: Williams' People's National Movement, later James' Workers and Farmers Party. Then, too, Williams' anti-communist de facto ban on James entering the country. I was to read C.L.R.'s *Black Jacobins* and his novel *Minty Alley* soon after. Maybe the difference was that C.L.R. recovered the resistance that people mounted against colonialism and slavery, and Williams spoke about the overwhelming nature of colonialism. A subtle difference and neither could be done without, but one dismissed colonial power as a decrepit apparatus in the whole sweep of history and the other let it in for too much contemplation.

Maybe the hint that some idea had not gone far enough in questioning colonial power interested me viscerally.

I know that it was twenty-four years later, after I had taken a plane to Grenada during the revolution, like my uncle but not just to see what was going on but knowing fully what was going on, to work at what was going on, that I met my uncle again. Again chasing his curiosity. This time he had taken a plane.

His first time in a plane, he told me, though it wasn't his first time in a fishing boat, the last time, when he had gone to Cuba to see what was going on when Fidel came down from the Sierra Maestra. I met him unexpectedly on the Carenage in St. Georges. This time he was not so virile but an old man, unshaved but unbearded. He wore a yellow shirt with stains on it, brown worn pants and a thin-brimmed straw hat, and he held a small brown bag on his left shoulder. He was walking along, near the small boats that went to Trinidad every Monday, Wednesday and Friday with agricultural produce. Trinidadians got uppity and stopped growing food when they got oil dollars, Grenadians liked to say. And Grenadians had a good hand with food growing. Well, he was walking along, finding his way to a guest house when I, walking to town, saw him. He wasn't looking for me. I don't think that he knew that I was there. I don't think that he knew that I remembered the story of his going to Cuba in a fishing boat. And I don't think that he knew that that is the story that probably led me to Grenada. I walked toward him incredulously, saying, 'Uncle, Uncle! What are you doing here?' He looked at me, unrecognising. After all, he had many nieces and nephews to remember, and he was so grand, though not so grand it seemed now, that I said, 'It's me, Dionne.' 'Ay, ay, but I don't know that?!' he replied. 'I don't know my own niece? Ay, ay, Dionne girl!' And he grinned, that grin, half-dangerous now, that he used to grin and his eyes still looking as if he were laughing at me. 'What you doing here?' I repeated, noticing that he seemed to have become small and thinking for a fearful moment that my family, the Brand mafia, had sent him to kidnap me out of Grenada as they thought that I was damn crazy to go to a revolution. And thinking that but remembering how my grand-father had said that Uncle was a damn fool to go to Cuba in a fishing boat, I heard him say, 'I come to see what going on here nah! They saying all kinda thing about the place so I come to see for myself.' 'How you reach?' I asked, settling into our language. 'Girl! Plane! I take the plane. The first time, you know! Girl! I frighten, frighten, frighten, when I tell you. Oh god. When it take off so I say lord what I doing this for? Where I going, eh? Ha god! But I close my eyes and I ain't look down yet, is so I frighten.' I could not stop laughing on the Carenage and he laughed, too, that grin laugh of his. 'But ent I had was to come? You don't find so?' Of course, we were comrades. 'But girl, the place ain't so much. Is what they talking about? I went to the zoo. It ain't have nothing there at all,' he laughed, 'two monkey and a parrot! You ever see thing so? But what they want with this place?' 'Is true, Uncle, but I glad to see you. You want to stay with me?' 'No, no, no, girl, don't worry with me. I have my business fix.' I had forgotten, looking at his less dangerous face, that when he was younger he was also considered a ladies' man. 'A lady have a guest house up so. Where you staying? I will call you.' With that Uncle left me on the Carenage and I didn't see him for the rest of his visit.

Well, I joined the revolution in Grenada in 1983, and I can still say that it was the best year of my life because it made the world finally seem right. Uncle had infected me, jumping into that fishing boat heading for Cuba, and nothing had felt right until getting there. Revolutions are not as simple as the words given to them after they fail or triumph. Those words do not account for the sense in the body of clarity or the sharpness in the brain, and they cannot interpret the utter vindication for people like me needing revolutions to reconcile being in a place. Why I went there was because I could not live in the uneasiness of conquest and enslavement, and it didn't seem to me that paths with even the merest suggestion of acceptance of these could lead me out. I could not choose to do anything else but fling myself at the hope that the world could be upturned.

The flat heat of poverty cannot fully explain this need, nor the chronology of awful events that is my history, but it is all this and the signs in my skin that keep me awake and alert.

I met the Cubans in Grenada. My Spanish was dreadful—I don't know how Uncle communicated with them back in 1959, but I didn't speak much. They were building an airport and some schools. Then there was the coup. Many of them got killed when the Americans invaded and the revolution ended.

And then a poet friend of mine said to me one June, 'I was so disappointed when I heard that you joined the Communist Party.' Her voice had genuine disappointment in it and, did I also detect, accusation. 'What about Stalin?' she continued. I paused, feeling slightly stunned at the passion in her voice and stopped walking along whatever green campus avenue we were walking and said, somewhat wondrous and taken aback, into a balmy Massachusetts night, 'But I was always heading there. It was inevitable, necessary.' I could not understand why she thought that invoking the name of Stalin would throw the whole matter into disrepute. Stalin, the blinding talisman that shuts out the light of an idea so profoundly human as the equal distribution of wealth, the free enjoyment of one's labour. There was no such talisman for capitalism, though. Truman, Kennedy, Nixon, Reagan, Bush, Verwoed,

Botha, Thatcher, Sukarno, Pinochet, the FBI, the CIA,
the capitalist industrialists, all these names, despite
the rivers of blood and pain running under them,
cloak themselves in the mystique of so-called
democracy, prosperity—and the blandness of their
terrors, their tortures, their massacres, their disasters
did not summon up any other passion but mine that
evening.

98

It was Uncle's freeness. Just like that up and took
a fishing boat to Cuba. I wonder what they thought
when they saw him. I heard they turned him back. I
know he landed at some small village that looked
like the village he came from. I'm sure he grinned
that grin at a woman who found herself feeding him
and trying to make out his smile. It was the way he
thought it possible or the way I thought he imagined
something beyond the same life. The way he went as
if going to a big event, a new place. He had style and
he felt his body living in any place he chose, he felt
it quicken at the thought of Cuba, he felt it move
across the sand toward the fishing boat. He felt his
hands loosen the rope, he felt his body climb over
the side and push off. He felt it dip and wave and
sicken into the sea, he felt it ignore its wretchedness
for imagining Cuba. He felt all of this not as separate
but as one movement from the time he heard it on
the radio to the time he saw Cuba. It was his sure-
ness that Cuba was where he should go, that seeing
Cuba was what he needed to do then. The coast

must have been well-patrolled, he didn't think of that; he would just be a nuisance, he didn't think of that either. He only thought of himself in Cuba in the middle of the revolution. I never asked him why he did it. If you looked at him you would know, and I didn't want his answer to complicate my imagination of him; he might have answered foolishly or vainly, said the wrong thing, or he may have changed his mind, thinking of it now as something his body once did involuntarily. Or he might have done it just to spite his father who thought that he was a damn fool for doing it. But truthfully, I didn't need it to be understandable or clear or even for what might be construed as the right reasons. He could have simply been curious.

Not even the headlines wide to half their page could dissuade me, though they did make my heart plummet, 'Communism Dead', 'Death of Communism', until I remembered the way most of the world still was. The headlines now trumpet the victories of the rich, the weakness of the poor, but I remember Cuba.

Brownman,
Tiger ...

So they don't stay home and cry to Martin Luther King movies or Malcolm X movies and grow stiff with loss, they're more restless. Sadness doesn't paralyse them. They're not immigrants so they're not grateful for the marginal existence they're afforded. They were born here, or they can't remember any place else; come to meet their mothers at three, four, ten years old. They've taught Italian boys and Portuguese girls to speak in patois and Bogle to Shaba. They've changed the accent on the buses going to Eglinton and Tretheway and Jamestown. They talk one language in the classroom and another at home; they think their mothers dupes for slugging it out in hospitals and nursing homes. They see a weakness in that and in the promises of making it. They've been roughed up, ground down and sidelined in this city's classrooms. Nobody knows what they really think and they're not saying except in the jammed-tight basement parties or dance hall parties with the metal detectors where they go anyway, strapped or carrying—boys and girls. They're not on the street like my generation before them; their view is inward, nursing wrath.

They're nervous and unhappy and they didn't read Fanon or Walter Rodney on the causes and the answers. In fact, when they came along Fanon was dead, Rodney had already been killed and a whole lot of Black people fighting for liberation in America, and their parents were scared, scared they wouldn't make it and scared that their children wouldn't make it, scared by all the killing—Malcolm X, Martin Luther King, George Jackson, Jonathan Jackson— and the imprisonments—the mass ones for just sitting or marching or being in the wrong place with the wrong colour, the other ones just for speaking, just for standing up, Angela Davis. Scared for just being Black.

When they came along what was left was the commercially altered remains of the sixties Black revolution, and anyone left in the house was working two jobs and just trying to stay alive. Now they heard mantra-like meaningless echoes of Malcolm 'by any means necessary' and took directions from record companies in the anointing of their new revolutionary leaders, Run DMC, Public Enemy ... well. Now the backlash went to work, melting down and

eroding whatever little got won. Now the revision-
ists went to work, the great legitimising machinery
of liberal democracy set about inserting itself as
always in favour of racial equality, selling it in the
popular culture, making movies—*Mississippi
Burning*, where the FBI led the Movement, and various other cinematic clones, and the racist idyll
Driving Miss Daisy, just to get things back to where
they were, Spike Lee's *Do the Right Thing*, just to say
that mass action was overreaction and foolishness
and responsible for tragedy.

The newspapers said immigrants were taking
away white people's jobs, the newspapers said Black
youth were running amok, the newspapers said
before Black people came here there was no racism,
the newspapers said before Black youth there was no
crime, the newspapers said we live in a multicultural society, the newspapers said when people come
here they just have to leave their culture behind and
become Canadian, the newspapers said multiculturalism was costing too much money, the newspapers
said soon there'll be more people of colour than
whites here, the newspaper said you had to be white
to be Canadian. Watching it all from the desolate
schoolyards and lunch-rooms and malls and public
high-rises in this city in the north that could barely
acknowledge their existence and fought hard against
giving them an equal education, denying the racism
in streaming them into the dead end of Level One

schools and holding long and endless discussions about whether they could really feel the insult of Little Black Sambo or whether they really needed to know their history, they took it in. In this city where ordinary educational fare for white children is begging special privilege for Black children, no wonder they're not satisfied with any Martin Luther King I-have-a-dream thing. In this city that now found their presence a nuisance, forgetting that it had imported their mothers by the thousands to work its kitchens and factories in the sixties and seventies. In this country that now found even their mothers superfluous and had actually told them not to bring along their appendages in the first place, the sand-lots are full of racial epithets that children must shrug off or be found too thin-skinned. In this city, Toronto the Good, that sets the police on them for hanging on the streets, for appearing in their own skins in malls and parking lots, and chases them down back alleys when they become so injured that they try to kill themselves with drugs rather than look at their image. Who can blame them for not believing anymore what's put in front of them? Can any white person imagine their whole teenage population being told that they're no good? Can they imagine the devastation of that statement coming from the mayor of the good city, the police chief of the good city and everyone with a gun in the good, good city? In this good city where they pile these mothers and

children up in low-ceilinged projects where your
heart squeezes into your throat and there's no room
to breath in the corridors, much less think yourself
out of this good, good city. Here they had an immigration hearing for a boy who came here at twelve
years old; they wanted to send him back. Never
mind they made him and he probably came here a
boy full of hope until they stuffed hopelessness
down his throat, until they told him he'd be a bas-
ketball star or maybe a football player or maybe he
could sing. Until they made him realise the only
options he had were superstar or criminal. Yes, some
gym teacher white and settling into his middle age
and wondering how he had not made much of himself, only enough to lord it over tall young Black
men, promising them the NBA and dreaming for
himself to be a superstar coach or perhaps not even
dreaming but fantasizing as he watches Phil Jackson
on TSN yell at grown Black men, fantasizing that he
was there, that he did not even have to be there to
tell those Black boys how to play because he was so
super-macho that he's more macho than seven-foot
Black men with arms spanning centre court. And his
fantasy makes up for all his life, but it needs a young
Black man, maybe twelve like Tiger, who could help
him dream of lifestyles of the rich and famous, and
it's a fantasy to get him by until retirement, but it's a
fantasy that doesn't let Tiger go until he is in the
doorway of some café like Just Desserts in Toronto

105

about to scare some people so that they are more scared than he, so that it drives his fear away.

Who else's children get so wickedly done by? And they even managed to indict a grandmother in Jamaica who Tiger allegedly grew up with. It's some old Black woman's fault. How far in their ever-surprisingly callow grab-bag of racist ideology did they have to reach for that one? Evil Black woman, ay. Dysfunctional Black family, what.

James Baldwin on the summer of his fourteenth year: 'It was a summer of dreadful speculations and discoveries. ... Crime became real for example—for the first time—not as *a* possibility but as *the* possibility. One would never defeat one's circumstances by working and saving one's pennies; one would never, by working, acquire that many pennies, and besides, the social treatment accorded even the most successful Negroes proved that one needed, in order to be free, something more than a bank account. One needed a handle, a lever, a means of inspiring fear. It was absolutely clear that the police would whip you and take you in as long as they could get away with it, and that everyone else would never, by the operation of any generous human feeling, cease to use you as an outlet for his frustrations and hostilities. Neither civilised reason nor Christian love would cause any of those people to treat you as they presumably wanted to be treated; only fear of your power to retaliate would cause them to do that, or to seem to do it, which was (and is) good enough.' [11]

How many young Black people in this city face a summer of 'dreadful speculations and discoveries', coming of age in a white society which wholly despises them and daily in the newspapers grafts on them its own fears, its own inability to conceive of any human life which does not look exactly like it? In 1979 I was working for the School Community Relations Department of the Toronto Board of Education. In a school in the east-end area that I worked was a seven year old who had got this city's destructive message. Each day he cowered under his desk or the teacher's desk, his face powdered thickly in the chalk dust from the blackboard. He didn't speak and no one could get him to come out from under the desk. This already ghostly child knew both the lesson of this society and his inability to accomplish it—that 'whiteness' gives you grace, blackness plunges you into madness if you follow the signs to their logical conclusion. In 1994, just as the robbery and shooting at Just Desserts ushered in the summer, every Black teenaged boy must have heard these dreadful speculations, these logical conclusions. This spring 'we' noticed and heard the dejection, confusion and slow realisation in the boy children that we share when the words 'Just Desserts' exploded into the category of descriptions for Black teenaged boys in this city, as policemen stared into their faces, stalked their stride, pulled them out of buses and off the sidewalks and warned the whole white city that any one of them can be it.

'What I saw around me that summer was what I had always seen; nothing had changed. ... Yet there was something deeper than these changes and less definable, that frightened. ... In the case of the girls, one watched them turning into matrons before they had become women. They began to manifest a curious and rather terrifying single-mindedness. It is hard to say exactly how this was conveyed: something implacable in the set of the lips, something farseeing (seeing what?) in the eyes, some new and crushing determination in the walk, something peremptory in the voice.' [12] Unfortunately, Baldwin did not extend himself beyond the flat misogynist image of girls turning into matrons, the underlying assumption being that ideally they should turn into women whom men would desire, that without the burden and distortion of racism they would achieve the highest hopes of their sex, that of fulfilling male desire. He did not plumb the possibilities of their recognition of the street that faced them, though he admitted in parentheses that he did not know what they saw. Perhaps his maleness and his fear for himself made him closed to their alternatives, leaving them only 'girl' or 'matron' or perhaps he rightly saw that matrons it would have to be, some finite prescribed position, if not the street. That it was equally fearful for them he did not acknowledge nor that for them protection lay in single-mindedness and sealing the air around their walk, affecting a matronly armour against 'the man' or any man and passing up on any whim to be carefree or free for that matter. What occurred to them was that suddenly they were prey to all and unimportant to everyone and if they were not careful they would end up pregnant or beaten up or on the walk. What happened was they suddenly faced taking care of everybody but themselves. Someone told them that this was how they would become worthwhile. Someone said, Step back now you were just made to be of service. And they had to put on a front, act as if they were in control of this sudden realisation, swallow it and digest it at once and feel it come hard and bitter before they even hit fifteen or withdraw resigned to waiting and watching life.

'You're nothing to them,' my niece said to me in May, talking about how she was trying to get a track scholarship to escape the Jane-Finch projects and that she knew that her grades had to be high because if she got hurt and couldn't run all the attention would disappear. Her voice had too much experience in it; she's only sixteen, her bones are brittle, she's had two fractures and a broken ankle, not enough calcium in a Jane-Finch diet. But she's running. Running fast and she is determined to be better than good, and her 'terrifying single-mindedness' is necessary because she knows much more than she ought to about the other side of it. She's walked too often through the mall, the emptiness, the fakery of its commoditised dreams, stood too often, asphalt-choked on one side of that too-wide intersection the cops patrol and listened too hard at the Christmas conversations of her aunts, one battered blue, another suicidal, crowded into the over-crowded living-room.

110

But perhaps Baldwin, like all of us then and now, left and right, Black and white, operated on the assumption of the given world as patriarchal, and that a challenge to manhood was therefore the final insult to the race or community. When that assumption is so riven through the actual and ideological life, what happens to males in the group becomes the measure of experience because we take whole-sale into our analysis the superiority and importance of male experience. Since the experience of patri-archy is mirrored in the world we are trying to fight, it is not inaccurate to say that unusual things happen to Black men and boys because they are men and boys, but it is a lie to say that nothing unusual hap-pens to women and girls because they are Black women and girls. Patriarchy makes us see what hap-pens to men as more offensive than what happens to women. So in my generation the pimps at the Le Coq D'Or, dressed in Afros and morning coats, inverted the Black revolution, exploiting women Black like them, telling them that they were Black men and the

world was against them and we Black women had a
duty to help them to get over, as desperate as we
were to find a place to get over ourselves. I used to
sit at Le Coq D'Or every Thursday, Friday and
Saturday night and at Sunday matinées, listening to
the funk bands from the States and watching the
pimps at the bar send Pink Ladies and Singapore
Slings to girls like me. It would have been a short
step from the inner pain to inclusion in this self-annihilating confidence game dressed up in liberation
rhetoric. There was not a night well into the wine
that I or my girlfriends did not think it possible. In
fact, we went to Le Coq D'Or to toy with the idea,
even though we saw women who had taken the bait
busted up, crying and bleeding at the hands of the
pimps. Le Coq D'Or offered us romance. The rhythm
and blues, the funk, created Black heterosexual
romance mythology. Wilson Pickett's 'When a Man
Loves a Woman' or 'I've Been Loving You Too Long'
validated our sense of Black desire, Black desire not
white desire as we had been fed and which derogat-
ed ours in the popular culture. We thought of names
for ourselves, too, Sweet D, Brown Sugar, Sweet
Nancy. We drank that elixir offered Black girls—an
iconography for Black desire, a system of signs and
ritual which would structure a community-defined
sexuality for a race as well as structure the relationships between men and women. Defined for so long
within white culture as outside of feminine norms,

we accepted a competing iconography of feminine sexuality within a taken-for-granted patriarchy. As well, we lived the double life of making it in the man's world in the jobs designated to us as Black women. There the average best we could become was a nurse or typist, exceptions notwithstanding, or the romance of Black desire would land us single mothers or on the walk.

Seen through the prism of patriarchy, romance is to women as action is to men. Violence or the threat of violence saturates, rationalises these concepts and also situates the racist acts of a racialised patriarchy within Black life. So young Black men in Toronto are shot by police and shoot each other at will today, and young Black women are brutalised, some get shot by cops, too, and answer to the names 'bitches' and 'hos'.

'It was real in both the boys and the girls, but it was somehow more vivid in the boys. ... And I began to feel in the boys a curious, wary, bewildered despair, as though they were now settling in for the long, hard winter of life. ... In the same way that the girls were destined to gain as much weight as their mothers, the boys, it was clear, would rise no higher than their fathers. School began to reveal itself, therefore, as a child's game that one could not win, and boys dropped out of school and went to work. ... My friends were now 'downtown' busy, as they put it 'fighting the man'. They began to care less about the way they looked, the way they dressed, the things they did; presently, one found them in twos and threes and fours, in a hallway, sharing a jug of wine or a bottle of whiskey, talking, cursing, fighting, sometimes weeping: lost, and unable to say what it was that oppressed them, except that they knew it was 'the man'—the white man. And there seemed to be no way whatever to remove this cloud that stood between them and the sun, between them and love and life and power, between them and whatever it was they wanted. One did not have to be very bright to realise how little one could do to change one's situation; one did not have to be abnormally sensitive to be worn down to a cutting edge by the incessant and gratuitous humiliation and danger one encountered every working day, all day long.' [13]

Baldwin might have been talking about 1994, but he would not have believed that we'd be still here and worse ... this cloud that stands between us and the sun, between us and love and life and power stands ever more pressing. We had expected it to be gone. We had promised it to this generation and so we cannot fault their nihilism and their loss of faith. We exist here at odds, at odds with life, at odds with love, at odds with power.

In another generation, my uncle's, they called themselves Icepick, Iceman, Priest and Atilla, fierce descriptions which took the boredom and morbidity out of hanging on corners, watching days pass them, and they had earned those names, too, with the use of a knife or ice-pick on other men like them, hanging on another corner; some of them came here to Canada after conversations on those corners about how it would be better, about how they could make money, break out of their colonial nightmare. In my generation we changed our names to Akua, Ayanna, Kwame, Kwetu, hoping that we could use the magic of these names, like garments made of stronger cloth to thread our way back through the portals of the slave castles, back to our true selves. But in my generation there was also Death who walked as if he were not alive and talked as slow as ice and raised a glacial eyebrow to anyone who said that dope would kill him and he was just giving in to the man, as if to say he was already dead, and I for one could never escape the knowledge in those eyes, so much so that I avoided him, pretending not to think anything of him.

Brownman, Tiger, are this year's names. Some take them in defence of themselves, some in self-pronouncement of the doom they saw and see, some to warn some evil away, some with self-deprecating humour, some with anti-hegemonic wit, some in complete hopelessness. No rescue for Brownman and Tiger here, though, in this city that treats its white rapists and murderers like the boy next door gone unaccountably and sadly wrong, no 'he was such a nice guy, you'd never think' for Brownman and Tiger; no wedding pictures of theirs plastered all over the newspapers, showing what a normal life they led. In fact, what the popular media would say was that Brownman had many girlfriends, playing to the stud icon of Black male sexuality, but Paul Bernardo, who is charged with the murders of at least two women and with multiple counts of rape, was the so-much-more-trustworthy, dream-boat, blond boy-next-door icon of white male sexuality, with the fairy-tale wedding. For Brownman and Tiger no week-long, sympathetic, emotional, trage-dian rumination on their mental state—were they 'distressed', like the white man who killed a two-year-old-girl, saying he was going to make her mother suffer forever? (You could swear they were talking about Macbeth or King Lear.) For them the hasty liberal judgement that no matter what, their crime was 'brutal' and 'heinous' and could never be understood. No label of white crime for all the white crime, no threats of sending white criminals back to where they came from. And wait, another euphemism in this good country, too good to say the word 'race', so it's 'immigrant', 'Jamaican', 'deporta-tion', because there would be no crime in this coun-try were it not for the 'immigrants', read Blacks, who should be deported to wherever they came from, right? And wait, another euphemism in this good country too good to say 'nigger', so it's 'crime'. Brownman and Tiger can't even do crime just like white folks and get treated just like white folks. Oh no, that wouldn't be enough. Every one of us has to walk around apologising to white people for getting on that ship we got shoved onto five hundred years ago, everyone of us has to apologise for the inconvenience of making white folks rich or privileged off our backs, we've got to apologise for still being around after we've been used up. The evidence of our skin is guilt enough for this good city. And we've got to pay for answering the ads to pick apples, clean house, sew sweatshirts, build cars, clean the sick, get a job paying more than you'll ever make in a tropical country with a Canadian bank on every corner. And we've got to pay for wanting to wake up just one single morning, any morning, left alone, without white people on our ass, messing around in that swill they made called racism, splashing it all over our desperate morning.

The truth is that North America does not need Black people any more; neither Canada nor the U.S. need the cheap labour assigned to our skins, and you can tell this by the slow criminalisation of social protest and by the difficult job of interesting a disaffected, cynical, commodity-sated white public in human rights and by the demonisation of the masses of Black peoples in North America on the television screens and in newspaper and magazine reports. They no longer need us for the cheap and degraded labour which we've represented across the centuries of our lives here. New technologies and the easy movement of capital through free-trade agreements and free-trade zones have eliminated the need for a work force in situ; then, too, since capital is based on scarcity and on little in for plenty out, even the minimal cost of social justice—equal education, equal pay, equal opportunity, etc.—is just too much of a bother and too expensive for trans-national capitalism. Why hire an empowered Black person in America when you can ship the work off to a less-enfranchised Colombian or Sri Lankan? Why empower a Black person in America to demand better wages and better working conditions? These conditions fill up the jails with unemployed, underemployed, unemployable. So an ideological war presages the economic war on Black people.

Perhaps Baldwin in the summer of his fourteenth year could find the church instead of the streets, but in whatever fourteen-year-old boy-child's or girl-child's summer this year is, not even the church is there for rescue, only the street, and it is full of cops and teachers and newspapermen and politicians only too willing to sacrifice them on the altar of their evil myth-making before they even come of age. No, not even the church awaits them and not even the dubious and soul-killing possibility of an exploitive job. These two thankless eventualities at least awaited James Baldwin and the other young people of his time and what awaited them, too, though they may not have known it, was their rebirth in the Civil Rights Movement. Even so, they counted on a notion that all people really wanted to be good to others, wanted to be just, wanted to share the world and would be redeemed by justice. This many years later an awful thought gains in strength and conviction: evil persists; justice is an idea for chumps. Civil rights ain't worth the hassle for white people. This many years later they don't have to pacify us with any toothless legislation, rather they ask, 'How are we to legislate behaviour?' meaning 'You can't force white people to be just.' Instead the new tactic (which smacks of the old tactic) is to dehumanise and terrorise Black people through police brutality and surveillance, to make sure that drugs are readily and cheaply available to our young people and to mount a massive and persuasive propaganda war on Black people in North America as a whole, labelling us drug addicts, criminals and whiners because we should have been able with the little that they gave us to turn ourselves into millionaires. Here a racist revisionism is in full swing in this country that never talks about race but about immigration and self-government, meaning people of colour and First Nations' people, meaning anybody who ain't white. They say that three hundred years is too soon for Native self-government. They say cut back immigration from countries that are not compatible with Canadian culture, meaning white culture. They say immigrants are taking away Canadian jobs, as if immigration is something altruistic and not about the economy and cheap labour.

Somewhere I worry about our souls because I know that after sixteen years of police killings and no convictions our eyes are dry and our young people cynical. They know what a cop sees when he sees them, thin as the outline of his shooting target. And one night one of them won't run down the alleyway with his dose of poisonous crack and the bullet heading for him. He'll turn all deadly and shoot, and we won't have the tears for anybody, not even for him.

'But now, without any warning, the whores and pimps and racketeers on the Avenue had become a personal menace. It had not before occurred to me that I could become one of them, but now I realised that we had been produced by the same circumstances. Many of my comrades were clearly headed for the Avenue, and my father said that I was headed that way too.' [14] This is the reason for our solidarity: no matter where we find ourselves in the outcomes of the system, we are all in the same jail, and we recognise the permutations, the desperation, in our acts to remove that cloud that stands between us and the sun, between us and life and love and power.

The second Rodney King trial, the morning of the verdict, two sisters and I are watching CNN at ten

o'clock in the morning. We're worried, feeling
unsafe, feeling vulnerable. These are the times that
Black people feel most unsafe, most vulnerable;
these are the times when we are almost one person,
when the next move that's made by anyone even
vaguely associated with power will determine the
conditions we'll live under, when some incident
happening to just one of us somewhere—doesn't
matter where—sends a warning to the rest of us to
watch out, take heart, panic, understand, take example, despair, be joyful …

Like the day Nelson Mandela got out of jail, and
I didn't have a television, and I couldn't wait for
clear morning to get out of bed and go to a friend
down the street to watch him. And when I got on the
street I felt like yelling and laughed out loud, called
out, in fact, to a young Black man putting junk mail
in mailboxes on Ossington that Mandela was out so
he should chuck the job, nothing was going to be the
same anymore, the world was changing that morning.

Now waiting for the second Rodney King verdict
was similar but different. The world was changing
that morning. If they were acquitted our lives would
be a greater hell; the three of us felt that, knew it. If
they were convicted, there would be some respite.
We sat on the couch tense, listening, watching. Each
conviction we punctuated with 'damn right, mutha-
fuckas!'

When the unrecognisable pictures of four young

men came on the television screens and the front
pages of the local and national newspapers we
flinched. In fact, we flinched even before that, listening for the descriptions, knowing that any crime
allegedly done by a Black person in this good city is
opportunity for white attacks, assaults from the
ever-present blame that white folks dole out univer-
sally. But we also flinched because we are waiting,
too, for the water to break, for the gush of rage to
envelop us in retaliation or self-hatred.

Water
More
Than
Flour

This phrase suddenly surprised me the other day, lit on my tongue when I didn't have any way to describe how I felt about the world that day. It just floated in, feather-like and perfect, as if it knew that I needed it. As if it knew that no other phrase would do. It struck me as vaguely familiar but seemed somehow anachronistic, and then I remembered where I had heard it before. The women in the community that I grew up in used an expression to characterise the state of the kitchen table, the state of their relationships, the state of the country, the state of the economy, the state of their purses, really, more keenly the state of the pot on the fire; water more than flour, they said, meaning that things were grim, bad, pretty near hopeless, money was tight or non-existent, hope was just a little short, ever so slightly beyond their imagination or recollection; water more than flour, they said, meaning they couldn't even make bread because flour was scarce and water in much more supply and water alone could not hold the dough together; water more than flour, they said, hand on their hip pensive and gently, always with a deep sense of knowledge, perhaps even of conviction. They said it, meaning nothing to eat, no sustenance; water more than flour, meaning that things were tough and would probably get tougher; water more than flour, to describe not only the physical but the spiritual state of want, meaning a thinness to life's possibilities, unerring hard times, an absence of joy, an absence of redemption or mercy or rescue.

More poetic, more expressive than any statement they could produce to say 'we are hungry and going to stay that way, and there are those out there who want us to be hungry, and we don't know when this is going to end, but it ain't right, and if we ever catch their ass it's going to be the big payback, but don't worry, god is going to take care of them.' Water more than flour was their way of finding some grace, the grace of a phrase, in the hunger, in the starkness, in the bareness in which we seemed destined to abide.

I often remember this, more and more these days. Within its textured meanings, it referred to the condition of being Black and female in the Americas. And I've been thinking about that these days, wondering if it's any different from their times, wondering if after the struggles of so many Black women I could say that it ain't so no more, wondering if I could get past that, and if it ain't so no more maybe I could pay some attention to returning phone calls, writing people back, getting used to my job, taking care of my stomach, oiling my skin, paying my bills or at least not being so scared when the bill collector calls. If it ain't so no more, maybe I could stop being so driven, stop thinking that every public or private gathering with white people is a war zone, stop thinking that every public or private gathering with men is a war zone, stop thinking that every public or private gathering with straights is a war zone, get used to the break up of the Soviet Union, believe that capitalism is really my friend, stop mourning Grenada and Nicaragua and Mozambique and every anti-colonial liberation struggle gone sour, stop thinking that there's an international racist conspiracy against people of colour, and it killed a Turkish woman and two Turkish girls in Germany, and it killed close to one hundred women and children, what it called 'combatants', in Somalia the other day, and it never did tell us how many Iraqis got killed in that war. If it ain't so no more, maybe, I could stop making these lists because I can't keep up, maybe I could stop being so suspicious, but just the other day I heard that the Canadian army is full of white supremacists and coloured men eager to prove themselves as brutal. That army killed two Somalis because that's what they went to Somalia to do.

Because, you know, it feels like water more than
flour because I can't seem to find room just to live
my life and just to pick up the phone and say hello
into it some days because in all of this I fear for my
Black woman's body, and I fear for it because just the
other day the *Toronto Star* emblazoned the words

'Gangster Bitch' over the face of Patsy Jones. Black
like me and twenty-one years old, she's the young
woman arrested as an accomplice in the murder of a
German tourist in Florida in August. In the nihilism
spawned in young Black people today in America,
in the deep self-hatred that is their piece of the
American pie, in the degradation fed to them like
bread, and in her most self-annihilating moment,
Patsy Jones nicknamed her young and innocent self
'Gangster Bitch', perhaps because she needed a fearsome name to beat the fearsome street that she knew
was gonna get her somehow, some way, any way,
and maybe she didn't know anything at all but just
repeated what she'd understood as the designated
ideological form of femininity for Black women on
this continent because America nicknamed all of us
'gangster bitch' a long time ago, and maybe the
equally nihilistic young men she hung with made
her say this name as duty for their company and tro-
phy for their own self-hatred, and for all these reasons she called herself 'Gangster Bitch'. But the *Star*
had none of those reasons. It reinscribed the words
'Gangster Bitch' over her head, over my head, and

gave them the structure of white ruling-class meaning, which locates Black women in the culture as
demonic, evil, worthless and sexually degraded. I
fear for my safety and for the safety of women like
me when I see 'gangster bitch' written over a Black
woman's face in the *Toronto Star*, and I fear for Patsy
Jones' inner life, a life already sacrificed to that
meaning, and I fear for my inner life which really
can't take too much more because I've been pretending that I can write my way out of it and all the
Toronto Star had to do to shake me was write 'gangster bitch' over a Black woman's face to bring me to
my knees.

And I fear for my Black woman-self because it
isn't just image or hollow ideology but because one
night, August 10th, to be exact, Audrey Smith felt
that meaning against her Black woman's flesh on the
corner of Dufferin and Queen in Toronto. Black like
me and woman like me, she was stripped-searched
on the corner of Dufferin and Queen. She was on
holiday from Jamaica. She was standing at the bus
stop near Dufferin and Queen when the police
approached her, accusing her of carrying drugs.
They threw her in the back of a police cruiser. She
protested, saying that she had no drugs and that
they could search her if they didn't think that she
was telling the truth. They took her out of the car,
made her get undressed at the corner of Dufferin
and Queen, made her stand naked at that busy

intersection, with passing cars and staring people, made her bend over, spread her legs, at the corner of Dufferin and Queen in Toronto just last week. When they were done and had found no drugs, just Audrey Smith's Black woman's body trying to find some rescue from their terror, when they were finished after re-enacting the terror of all of Audrey Smith's foremothers and mine, stripped just so, degraded just so, they got into their cruiser and drove away, leaving Audrey naked and violated at the corner of Dufferin and Queen.

Water more than flour, the women in my family would say, but this time they would say it bitter-like and ready to kill somebody.

Last night I saw a woman standing at the corner of Oakwood and St. Clair, it was around 8:30 and she was waiting for someone. She was the kind of woman I knew from just looking at her, the skirt to just below her knees, the white shirt ironed, the hair permed, the shoes patent-leather and backless. She worked in a factory, I was sure, maybe shift work, maybe she came home tired or went to work tired, she stood trying to be invisible against the street, she almost crouched, stooped, trying to attract only the attention of whomever she was waiting for, trying not to suggest any other possibility to passing white motorists or white men standing across the street, but I saw her and recognised that look of not calling attention to your Black woman-self on a street corner at 8:30 at night, waiting for a lover perhaps or more likely your girlfriend to go to the movies or bingo or church, dressed in her plaid decent skirt, hiding any evidence of sensuality, girdling it down. Because you could be labelled 'gangster bitch' or get strip-searched, and 'nice' white people will act innocent and flabbergasted, and Black men on the CHIN radio will ask you again and again where did they touch you and they say someone, your saviour, passed by and said you had a fat what ...

I idled the car after the lights went green for me to go, looking at her. I wanted to touch her, to shake her, tell her we were all right and one day we'll stand on a street corner with no shame or fear or trepidation, with no white words hanging over us or white cops waiting to strip us naked and degrade us, and she won't have to hide herself in a plaid skirt or the perm she had done to make herself look white, we won't have to erase ourselves from the world, or try to be invisible in order to live in it. But of course I could give her no such reassurance. Not only because racism is so powerful but because I'm a dyke and she's probably straight and that passage between us is full of fears, too. And her permed hair and her nice lady-like below-the-knees-skirt shows that she's trying to make it and she doesn't need me to give her away. Right now, being straight is the only thing she's got going for her, the only thing that she can safely do that would look normal in this very white, very male, very heterosexual place. How did Barbara Smith say it? 'Heterosexual privilege is usually the only privilege that Black women have. None of us have racial or sexual privilege, almost none of us have class privilege; maintaining "straightness" is our last resort.' And days later I wondered was she the woman whose two year old was screaming for her on the front page of the following afternoon's paper because her husband had shot her to death on Driftwood Avenue. The two-year-old girl-child weeping, white ribbons in her hair, and have mercy! in the arms of a white cop, frightening me, thinking she looked so much like my niece and what's going to happen to her in this country, thinking I'm gonna find the money and send my niece to a Black country to grow up in and thinking, yeah, but where am I going to find a Black woman country to send her to?

I know I have to find a Black woman country because if they came for Patsy Jones and Audrey Smith and the woman on the corner and the little girl screaming in the newspaper, and they had tried to follow the rules, then they'll be coming for me soon because I'm a Black woman who loves women and by their reckoning, well ... you know what that means in terms of gangsterism, so I have to find me a Black woman country real quick ... because water more than flour here.

Nothing
of
Egypt

After Grenada I came home to a city that seemed impregnable in light of what I had just seen. Devastation, physical and political. Ottawa looked wickedly concrete. I grudged its girded self-satisfaction, envied and hated its square, squat contentment. It looked like a fortress in comfortable repose, the ground hard, the blood frozen in the cool river veining through it. The thought occurred to me that nothing could shake it, no one would ever bomb it regardless of its Cold War fantasy as a target, its military congregations and its pretences. Coming back, I felt more defeated than I had crouched into a muscle in the corridor where I'd spent most of the five-day war. The place I'd just been was vulnerable, the buildings felt temporary despite their attempts to hold government and destiny and resolve. I recall looking out at American helicopter gunships strafing the offices of the Prime Minister one afternoon of the war. The building hung tenuously to a hill green from the rainy season. This day the sky was a dazzling white, the sun making the clouds silver and the American gunships like bees stung the building and the hill. The air seemed molten and the helicopters spewed metal, thickening the porous air white, leaving the ground bottomless. The building caught on fire and burned after they were gone and all night long. From the verandah, where I stood limp against the wall, the ricketiness of the Third World fell as my heart's own. The sun sank lightning-white into the ocean at the harbour and I stood watching it go, my face on fire.

This is why I do not believe in magic anymore. This is why my ancestors fail me with all their chants and potions. Because I wanted that day to rain sheets of water which would cover the island. I wanted a day when the enemy would be so overwhelmed by the sound of my ancestors dragging their chains that they would be killed by the clamour. I wanted a day when they would be compelled by that same spell which enveloped me, and their weapons would seize up or they would run away with screams in their heads. And at least if that did not happen I wanted to die. But this is why I had to find a theory instead of a powder because I didn't die and the ancestors only have mouth for me, not for American bombers.

The city I returned to, my face still burning,

would never collapse like this, I knew, and it was more than coincidence. In this city I returned to without a country, without a home, I recognised the grim geography of latitude and longitude, the bitter circle of almanacs, like someone stuck in a life living itself over and over and over again.

I remember this because someone asked me where I'd been, what happened to me after that, why hadn't I returned and slipped back into the friendships, the talks, the steady beat of the world the way it was. And lately I've been thinking about the last twenty-five years, which included this homecoming and many leavings, remembering when I went missing, when I decided to jump time, when suddenly I could not believe or accept the odd and stupid rhythm of what stands for living. Let me put it more plainly. Sometimes you go to bed at night and lie in your bed in the corner of some room, and just before sleeping the room seems larger, the distance to the door longer and your body smaller than it is, and you try to refocus your eyes to the room's right proportions, but it doesn't work and staring longer only makes the room bigger. It is some kind of optical trick that your eyes play on you, and you realise that if not for some tissue in your retina correcting everything, regulating your looks, you would see the world differently, or the world is different if not for that. So when I came home the world looked like this and I woke up the next morning and it kept looking this way and I was glad and I held on to this look.

I went to the funeral of a veteran woman fighter for civil rights in this city. The room took me back to when I joined the struggle in earnest. People I had not seen in a decade, people I had worked with, people I had forgotten. It was almost like twenty-five years ago except that everyone looked weary. Some looked prosperous, some beaten down, some resigned, but all weary. Because whatever decision you take—capitulation or tenacity—fighting against racism, living with racism takes a physical toll. So we all looked weary. I sat in the balcony of the church, watching the congregation as if watching the door of my room, and something struck me when the eulogies were said. It surprised me that ringing through them was the idea of upliftment, and I realised that at some point the idea of upliftment had replaced the idea of justice and that equality rather than justice had become what we were fighting for. The distinction may seem slippery, but it is a major one. Did we want only to be equal to white people or did we want to end exploitation and oppression? Because to be equal to the white power structure twenty-five years ago and still today is to have the right to impose inequality. Did we just need a good education and good jobs as the eulogies intoned? Some of us got a good education and got good jobs, but racism continued. In retrospect, the power structure has only used us to point out that those of us who don't have good jobs are just low-life after all. Were we low then and just in need of upliftment, or were we downtrodden by an economic system that depends on racism for profit? Surely merely to be uplifted means to accept the conditions of exploitation and oppression and to hold yourself an exception within it. To fight for justice is to eradicate those conditions completely. Well, somewhere along the line the notion of just going for piece of the pie had taken a hold. Watching those faces at the funeral, I tried to figure out when and how. Perhaps because for the most part we were an immigrant community who, fleeing hard times in the Caribbean or rather pushed to and fro by the exigencies of capital's need for cheap labour, had for the most part come to find a 'better way of life' and were therefore more prone, with the exception of a few committed radicals, to accept in part the way things were. Did this then lead to the conservative notions of equality? Were the radicals overwhelmed by this tendency as much as by the tendency of the capitalist state to co-opt some form of our claims of racial inequity into its bureaucracy? Definitely. Hadn't I lived through the obscuring of any right-left distinctions in the community just because we found ourselves in the same room and racism up in our face. We didn't want to quarrel publicly or lose any of the so-called gains of the struggle by showing white people that we disagreed on the way forward. So the Black left was trapped in that same silence that Black women are trapped in, the silence of unity.

And during the eulogies, the long, dispassionate descriptions of a woman, any Black woman, the usual words: strong, capable, steadfast. Among these, a poem read by a young woman, Eva's daughter. A simple declaration of love for her mother, no, nothing so ordinary as love but recognition of her mother. She said no other words but the poem, left us startled and wordless from its honesty. It said that everyone saw her mother as strong, forbearing, hardworking and that was true, but she said, 'I see a woman of tears.' I don't know how we all continued after that, and I had to leave before the service ended but not before this glimpse was closed, this seam sewed over in that way we have by words, the same words about this Black woman—strong, capable, steadfast. Yet the poem lay open like a vein running red in the black-robed solemnity of the Shaw Street Black church.

They were vibrant and hopeful days, the seventies. We argued, we debated, we came into the joy of being Black, we discovered parts of ourselves that we didn't know existed. And, yes, I was a woman feeling the discomfort of the sexual politics which dictated men as the leadership and women as the helpers even as the actual workings of the movement belied this hierarchy. I was a woman seeing the sexual capital of the radical men played out in the subjugation of women. So the movement was far from perfect, but just as I heard the call for a cultural nationalism that proscribed women's leadership except at home, I also heard that the struggle was not a struggle for the petty gains of privilege the system will give, as the system gives what reinforces it. And I also heard that we had to move beyond individual aspirations and retake the vision we had created first in the goals of emancipation and liberation. That vision was, after all, something about the possibilities for human existence. We, as a people, over the last five hundred years had engaged this world in the most crucial argument of human history—that of the nature of human beings and of human freedom. It was more than enough to hold me in the movement, despite the uneasy feeling that Black women's experiences were secondary and that men exemplified the voice, the life, the physical body and spiritual breath of the movement. And even more, one had a sense that male power over women was a prerequisite and a condition of the movement. The movement did not examine patriarchy. It examined white patriarchy but only as something that white men did to Black men not as something that men did to women, and in this it deserted its highest goals: freedom from all exploitation and oppression.

Even with this, it was more than enough to lead me to Grenada. On my way there this is where I had come from. I could not abandon my legitimate stake in freedom. Somewhere, despite the call to weakness, I had the idea that ultimately the struggle would allow me to operate for my own human self. That I was not the only woman going off to a revolution, for herself, convinced me that I was not alone in this. That it would be possible at the end to break the image of the strong Black woman we always hear about in the struggle for everyone else but herself. But I cannot say that it was all this clear then, climbing into the plane coming down at that tiny airport whose small ambition would lead to the American invasion. But I felt it in my skin. Revolutions do not happen outside of you, they happen in the vein, they change you and you change yourself, you wake up in the morning changing. You say this is the human being I want to be. You are making yourself for the future, and you do not even know the extent of it when you begin but you have a hint, a taste in your throat of the warm elixir of the possible.

It was some time in that house over the harbour where six comrades and I waited to be bombed, days when I thought about what I would do if I got out, days when I pitched like a drunk between wanting to die quickly and dreadfully wanting to live. It was only five days, but they took a long time to pass. I could hear each minute's temporal hum and the hum of the blood in my head. The skin burns. And the jaw clamps tight. And the mouth tastes like

paper but sour. I could do nothing but think and
notice the independence of my body and the disloy-
alty of the region of my brain which keeps notes on
the present. I could do nothing but think because I
could not sleep. Think, interminable minute after
interminable minute.

Here, look, it has always seemed impossible to
talk or write about this because so many people
lived it and many were injured more, more painful-
ly because colonial war is physical and mental harm,
so many that I hesitate to write because writing is
claiming all the pain and I cannot claim all the pain
and because luck and being able to—like a writer—
carve out a place where pain is transcended, like the
place in that corridor during that war where I cut
myself a muscle from my back and said I would survive as this. So each time I speak I must say mine
was not the only terror and not the most important
but a small thing in my small self compared to the
hundred thousand crouching in the other houses,
their fate slipping. I might reach another city with a
passport and a fortress and a sanguine river with my
face aflame, with the wrong answers, wishing that
I'd been killed but at least certain, however dreadfully, that I was only wishing.

I could do nothing but think. Sum up. In the time.
With all in me quartered and pulled apart but everything becoming clear as flesh, every face readable,
every moment distinct. If I had ideas before, these

days made them into blood, acts one cannot live with anymore if one lives, compromises one cannot make any longer, speeches one cannot sit for. And desires, they come apart, break off to the bone. Everything is naked and not in the least bit startling. The true length of the room appears. Your eye has perfect clarity, utter clarity, and you think how petty the earth is, how domestic, how small-minded and when can I leave and what in hell am I doing here.

When I came home I could not dance. All the funk was gone and what had been the effortless joy of the body swinging among other bodies against seventies R&B—that all fled. Dancing lost its naturalness. I couldn't do it without comrades. Where I had found comradeship in Saturday night dances on St. Clair Avenue and at Hagerman Hall, where I had found comradeship in the involuntary physicality of the Black dance floor, where I had found comradeship in the new move, the new walk, all the distillation of a common life in visceral joy, this comradeship was suddenly not enough. Or at least when I tried to rejoin it in the same way, I failed. I wonder if they couldn't dance in Grenada for so many months after or for so many years. How a war can seize your limbs, your sense of rhythm. How it can say if you dance, move one tendon to a pattern, you betray those who died or were lost; you act as if nothing has happened and nothing needs to be mourned.

'When I left the house of bondage, I left everything

behind. I wasn't going to keep nothing of Egypt on me, and so I went to the lord and asked him to give me a new name. And the lord gave Sojourner, because I was to travel up and down the land, showing the people their sins, and being a sign unto them. Afterward I told the lord I wanted another name, 'cause everybody has two names; and the lord gave me Truth, because I was to declare the truth to the people.'

How she must have felt, her face clear as that answer, with nothing at her back that she might want to turn and look at, how without sentiment for evil or grief she walked into her self.

Nothing of Egypt on me. No, nothing of Egypt. When I came home from Grenada I understood this. I wanted nothing of Egypt on me. How do I describe that feeling of freedom that you get when you don't die. Something says, 'I don't have to take anything anymore, nothing has power over me.' And even if years pass and you forget and sometimes you are afraid, the notion stays with you. Just this thought, nothing has power over me, causes you to change even more. In a strange way the revolution is complete in you and you can do anything. What's more, it says you must turn over completely, everything is in question. No matter how far you thought that you had gone there is further. Nothing of Egypt on me. Heading for a revolution is heading for your true self. I began leaving the house of bondage when I arrived in Grenada. Just being in the revolution, walking those hard hills, was walking out of bondage. My feet moved fast in the days there. I learned patience and I remembered desire. The patience of the eyes taking in the road to Gouave, the women fixing stones to it, the slick tar, the unbearable sun. The desire for the sight of the drop to water at Sauteres, the milk of ocean at Petite Martinique, how a woman digging yams in the bush can emerge, hands big as night. Things fell away, the slough of patriarchal life, the duty of female weakness, the fear that moves it, the desire grafted to it. And when the morning came that the American airplanes were in the sky, this knowledge had become tougher and tougher, toughening in the shape of a woman who was me and whom I desired and … I dreamed off, looking at the door of the room.

An old friend who was perhaps never a friend but a man in the only way he knew how to be a friend said to me in a bar on Queen Street, the other night, 'What happened, man, what happened? You disappeared from the scene, you were … you know, you did the poetry and pan thing, that was way back, man. And I gotta tell you, I don't understand the lesbian thing.'

'Well, you know, man, the first thing. I wasn't going to learn music, see, and so I didn't feel right. I know, I know, but I had to be committed to learning it, so I couldn't do the poetry and pan thing anymore.

I had to know everything about the form I didn't just want ... and music didn't interest me. I wanted only the words man. Man, if I could tell you, things changed, you know.'

'Yeah, Grenada, I know but ...'

'Yeah, Grenada, man, you know ... things just changed. My life changed. I'll call you. We'll talk.'

In a hallway on the morning when the American airplanes come and you are a muscle crouching in on itself you think of all the reasons why you are in the struggle and so, yes, of course you disappear from a certain life, you are released into another, and you do not call anyone to explain because the world is new and there are no lines of talk across.

Whose Gaze, and Who Speaks for Whom

Watching the film *Round Midnight* at the Bloor Cinema. Dexter Gordon, the saxophonist, plays a character loosely based on the life of Lester Young. 'A great shambling ruin of a man,' as the film promo reads, Gordon's character is befriended by an adoring white Frenchman whose love of this jazz great leads him to follow Gordon's character back to New York and through his life on the seedy side of jazz— the sleazy managers, the clubs, the drug habit, the genius ... The film locates its point of view and therefore ours in the white man who screens and translates the fatalist jazz virtuoso. The white Frenchman is the conduit, the cipher through which Black genius is explained. The audience sees Gordon in oblique long shot, in rheumy-eyed, gelled close-up, sitting in a dingy room slurring or muttering to himself or to the white man. And then again we see him in the purity of his performances, themselves studies in ruin, and moments of opacity, disappearance into sound. We are made to watch Gordon through the white man ... Gordon is tragic and gifted, 'Negro' and god-like, helpless and powerful, mumbling idiot and sheer genius. Though the white man is totally superfluous—he himself is not situated in any time or place but is a kind of universal transparency, his eyes registering tolerant affection, pity, grief, fatal knowledge as the camera makes us watch him watch Gordon—he is nevertheless our gaze, our way to understand Gordon's character who never speaks to us directly but only through the suffused benevolent light of the white man's eyes. Only through this intervention into representation, a screen decentring Gordon as the subject of his life, are we allowed to identify Gordon, and we can only identify him as an approximation and not an actuality of the human presence. The human presence is the white man's benevolent, universal eye, and Gordon is the object of his arbitrary and unending verification and correction for human similitude. Clearly, I was not the audience that the film had in mind, for the audience is constructed through the white man's eyes—his knowing looks communicate with another knower outside the screen. Together— the Frenchman and some generic white audience including this Anglo-Canadian one—they know something that Gordon doesn't. They construct

Gordon as an object of pity and doom. In her essay 'Representations of "whiteness" in the Black Imagination' bell hooks tells us 'issues of mere recognition are linked to the practice of imperialist racial domination.' Sitting in the audience, I feel under scrutiny; I, too, feel his gaze and the gaze of the knower communicating with the screen. I identify this gaze as the gaze of liberal racism, which codifies Black genius as tragic but somehow energising for the white man who steps into 'agency' at the genius' dissolution. I feel dissolute myself under the gaze of the audience as I leave the theatre.

At the Backstage Cinema on Balmuto Street in Toronto one night, I watch a documentary about Thelonious Monk. The audience was white, except for my partner and I. They are jazz aficionados. Monk pirouettes, spins and spins in the dressing room, the train station, the tour bus ... he spins and smiles and giggles and is serious ... the audience at the Backstage laughs. My partner and I watch Monk go mad. The more Monk spins the more the audience laughs. I wonder what they're laughing at. It is as if they think that his madness is part of his performance, put there to please them. They laugh as if they are in the know with Monk, the way a jazz audience snaps its fingers or nods its head when a performer is kicking it. I just see something so vulnerable it hurts to watch. I just watch Monk go mad and listen for how this movie says nothing about why. Not a word about the shape of blackness in America; not a word about Monk's mother—did he have a sister? what was the street that he grew up on? did he like roast beef? for example. I listen to them dip their laughter into Monk's sickness with America as if they're tasting chocolate. Finally I am so angry and so sad for Monk and I that I yell out in the cinema, 'What the hell is so fucking funny!'

At Norwich in England I am on a tour of Canadian women writers. When we arrive we find our rooms and then decide to get something to eat. As we step toward the nearest outside pub, a group of white young men point at me and begin to laugh, drawing me to the attention of others in the pub. So far I've been unable to find another Black face in town. Later after the readings we go to the best restaurant in town. The walls are covered in posters of John Coltrane, Ella Fitzgerald, Billie Holiday, Dexter Gordon, Randy Weston, Dinah Washington, Charlie 'Bird' Parker, Cecil Taylor, etcetera, etcetera … I note the consumption of Black people by white audiences from Toronto to Norwich. Bird is playing as we eat. Another writer at the table asks me how racism makes me feel. Morally superior, I say without hesitation, surprising her. It is not about how I feel, I tell her. I am more fearfully concerned with the kind of character who practises racism, who contemplates, designs and executes it every day until it becomes casual, common-sensical. This is the character of a torturer.

A Blues Festival at Harbourfront, last summer,
Pinetop Perkins, ninety-three years old, blues piano
player. I sit through a number of tedious blues
pianists to get to hear Pinetop Perkins play. It is a
blues piano workshop. The rest can't play worth a
damn, so my lover and I have a beer and wait. She
sucks her teeth after every pretender. One young
woman pianist is talking about how she mixes the
twelve-bar blues with European classical, then she
fields a question from the audience. The audience,
by the way, in the Brigantine Room is mostly white,
so are the blues pianists except for Pinetop Perkins.
Someone asks when did blues piano develop, as she
says, 'beyond the twelve-bar blues'. She replies, stu-
pendously, 'When Freud and Jung discovered more
about the human psyche over in Europe all that
thinking had an influence on blues music.' My lover
and I let out a loud, simultaneous 'Puhlease!' Like
Freud discovered the Mississippi Delta, like he set
up a couch in a buffet flat in Chicago! Pinetop finally comes on, humbly suggesting that really he didn't
know much about music but he'd learned to play by
ear and he'd composed a few pieces and they sound-
ed like this ... and he'd loved the blues all his life
and it was just that simple. He had stories about who
he'd learned what licks from and which were his
own and when he composed what and how lucky he
was to play the blues. Perkins is signifying on the

white pianists he's just heard. Only one of them bothers to acknowledge the history of blues—he even says the words 'Black people', unlike the others. Something tells me that Perkins decided to read all that appropriation into a simple statement on honesty and accountability.

There's another racialised dynamic happening here. Pinetop Perkins is being used as the racial foil in the blues workshop's writing of race relations and inter-racial encounter. He is an old blues man, and in a Black community of blues players and blues audiences his virtuosity would be accorded veneration and context as a kind of historical speech in a continuum, a language sent and understood and in action. At the blues workshop, Perkins is suspended in time, out of context, preserved as a museum piece, an icon no longer charged with readiness, place, dynamism, no longer seen as acting but as inert, a remnant of a dead—or rather a conquered—culture. Frantz Fanon once said that this is how European culture likes to see the culture of those it has conquered, as sentiment rather than meaning or action. So at the blues workshop there were no contemporary Black blues pianists to spoil the white mediation of Black culture as petrified in time, full of 'ancient' sorrow but no present disturbing anger and certainly no hostile intent.

Invited to a panel on cultural appropriation at the University of Toronto on 'Who Can Speak for

Whom', I decide to lay it out straight; I'll say it plain.
Look, this appropriation shit is not about me. It's just
for liberal white folks (not conservative ones 'cause
they're honest, crude really about what they're trying to do from the jump), getting upset that maybe,
just maybe, they oughtta check out what they're saying before they say it, and maybe, just maybe, they
don't know what the hell they're talking about when
they talk about anybody who ain't them. That's their
problem. I don't play that. We figured this shit out
since the sixties. Didn't white people ever hear about
cultural imperialism? Must be some kinda amnesia
going round, or else this is the most simple-minded
nation on the planet, or they're into some serious
denial. But it ain't my problem 'cause if somebody's
stealing stuff from me, I'm sure as hell not going to
go tell them that maybe they didn't notice but their
hand is in my pocket, 'cause both me and them
know what's really going down. I don't feature that.
Take that innocent bullshit some other place or else
admit you're lying and you damn well know what
you're doing. But the bottom line is the whole run
down ain't about changing nothing; it's about justi-
fying the status quo. Conservative or liberal, they
believe that the society is fundamentally just, and
they believe their history justified, so when we come
along and suggest that it ain't so they all jump on the
defensive. Like, the conservatives say: let's put on
Showboat, it's our heritage, it's a classic, for god's

sake! We say: classic my ass. Classic racism, huh? Classic white interpretation of slavery, classic white romanticization of that brutal institution, classic white heterosexual fantasy predicated on Black servitude. It's classic all right. Now the liberals, who pose as opposition, say: well, while it is an unfortunate choice now, it's censorship *not* to put *Showboat* on. I guess we probably infringed on somebody's right to own property when we rebelled against slavery. All boils down to the same thing. Liberal or conservative, it's classic white supremacy. Pieces of the past are always swept away in search of a more humane society. What makes this piece so hard for white people to let go? With the wide range of possible productions for a publicly funded arts centre in North York, a community with a large Black population, what Freudian psychosis made them choose *Showboat?* White racial memory, I say. Nostalgia, a deep longing for a racist past.

Well, it was too much trouble to say all that. So who can speak for whom? Some part of this text we are about to make is already written ... that I am a Black woman speaking to a largely white audience is a major construction of the text. blackness and 'whiteness' structure and mediate our interchanges—verbal, physical, sensual, political—they mediate them so that there are some things that I will say to you and some things that I won't. And quite possibly the most important things will be the ones that I withhold. The racialised power relations that we live determine what I will say and how I will approach my saying it. Our relative positionings within the society are at the core of these determinations. Notions of voice, representation, theme, style, imagination are charged with these historical locations and require rigorous examination rather than liberal assumptions of universal subjectivity or the downright denial of such locations. Even if my audience here were half Black or three-quarters Black, even if it were fully Black or people of colour, blackness and 'whiteness'—racial identities—would still mediate our conversation, though in such circumstance I might become a little more revealing. In such circumstances so much time wouldn't be wasted in convincing white people that their 'ruling' culture firstly, exists, secondly, was and is violently invasive and hegemonic and rationalises all others it meets into subordinated categories. That is, we might and in full cognizance of these circumstances proceed beyond white ignorance, white denial, white fear, white apathy, white lies, white power disguised as concern for censorship. Whites, that is, might proceed into the dangerous territory of knowing, instead of engaging in the sleight of hand that Michelle Wallace calls 'the production of knowledge (that) is constantly employed in reinforcing intellectual racism.'

It's a curious, curious thing that Canada is only

153

just now struggling with this question. It's even more curious that I would have practically grown up here in a Black community that struggled against cultural imperialism back in the sixties and seventies yet white Canada remained strangely immune to that intellectual debate until now. That this is so attests to the divided interests of white and Black communities in this country.

This from Michael Valpy of the *Globe and Mail*, May 4, 1993, 'Exactly a year ago, white and black youths rampaged along Toronto's Yonge Street, smashing shop windows, looting and indulging in other forms of mayhem. We will never know exactly what set it off. The event did grow out of an anti-racism demonstration earlier in the day focused on the Rodney King case in Los Angeles. However, subsequent exploration (plus the presence of as many white youths in what the news media too instantly labelled "racial unrest") suggests that what took place was more young discontent and rowdiness—period—than young black discontent.'

We will never know what set it off. Valpy is probably one of the most liberal columnists at the *Globe* so this account on the anniversary of the 1992 Yonge Street insurrection tries to be 'even-handed' in passing out the 'blame' that right-wingers assigned to a 'pathological' Black community. He makes sure to mention that there was 'smashing' and 'looting' and 'mayhem' (this assures the right that he is not going soft on disorder) which, he says, should not be so 'instantly labelled "racial unrest"' (this assures the nation that racism is not a problem here). And then he concludes even more reassuringly that it's just 'young discontent and rowdiness' which of course we can all understand and go back to sleep because it'll pass. *We will never know what set it off.* Oh the wonder and deliberateness of liberal dissembling!

Well, I was there, honey, and let me assure you it was racial unrest. I felt it myself, the imperative to tear down all manifestation of a system that keeps its foot at our throat, saw it on the faces of the young Black people on the street, was proud of them for standing up and sending a message to this country about not taking it anymore, felt repudiated like many of the older activists on the street; we hadn't done enough so that they wouldn't have to go through this. We had not succeeded in wiping out racism; we had not succeeded in over a decade of trying to stop police killings of Black people and police brutality. They were taking it to the street. All we could do was tell them, and they often listened, that looting is not a political act. All we could do was tell them not to get arrested for the wrong thing, but we could not nor did we have it in us to tell them to wait and justice would come. Yes, there were white youth in the demonstration, some in solidarity, some for their own beef with the police. It's amazing how the powers-that-be never expect or think people capable of solidarity with each other, never expect or think people capable of making connections between the way certain groups are treated. And it is a sign of their confidence in racism that they never expect white people to act against white ruling-class interests. So if this happens they must find another explanation—general youthful discontent, not a sign

of political consciousness and solidarity.

And 'what set it off'—such innocence! What Valpy omitted unaccountably was the police brutality that Blacks endure in this country. Incredibly, he omitted that a week or so before the Yonge Street insurrection two police officers accused of killing a Black teenager, Michael Wade Lawson, in Peel Region, were exonerated. (Lawson had been shot in the back of the head.) He further omitted that two days after the Los Angeles verdict and insurrection, Toronto police shot and killed yet another Black man, Raymond Lawrence. He failed to take into account ten years of protest against police beatings, shootings and killings of Black people in Toronto. He failed to notice ten years without a single conviction of a police officer and he failed to notice the image on national television of the white officer acquitted in the Lester Donaldson killing, a victory cigar in his mouth, triumph over and disdain for Black people on his face, smiling for the cameras.

Invited to several more panels on cultural appropriation, I decline. Too busy fighting small things.

My partner and I got hauled over and searched at the Toronto airport coming back from a reading in Trinidad. The other people getting searched are just like us. Every encounter with immigration is layered in racism so I hate leaving the country. A month later, my partner gets strip-searched at the Rainbow Bridge. Cross-border shopping might be okay for white folks, but it's a cross-border hazard for us. They don't believe that she was born in Nova Scotia; all Blacks are recent immigrants and always suspect. That's just at the borders. Inside the perimeter it gets worse. My nephew's getting screwed in school. I'm worried. Every Black kid's getting screwed—they're classified as either behavioural problems or as learning-disabled. A Somali friend wants to know what to do about her child. The teacher says he's a thief— he's stealing other children's opportunities by shouting out the answers before the other kids. He's six years old. Inside the perimeter it gets dangerous. Skin-heads chase after my Korean friend one night on Spadina. I tell her don't walk out there at night. She says don't be ridiculous. And it gets petty. My ex-lover is followed with suspicion through the women's locker-room at the Y. The group of women following her tell her nastily that she has to shower before going into the pool. Thousands of us scrambling around every day fixing this, making do and taking that—well, cultural appropriation is not on the short list.

But speaking about cultural imperialism, and 'post' everything aside, post-colonialism and post-modernism, I am gratefully reminded of Amilcar Cabral's clarity. In *Return to the Source* he said, 'History teaches us that, in certain circumstances it is very easy for the (imperialist) to impose his domination on a people. But it also teaches us that whatever may be the material aspects of this domination, it can be maintained only by the permanent, organised repression of the cultural life of the people concerned. ... Thus it is understood that imperialist domination, by denying the historical development of the dominated people, necessarily also denies their cultural development ... imperialist domination requires cultural oppression.'[15]

This is the more precise term: 'cultural imperialism'—'the permanent, organised repression of the cultural life of the people concerned'. Several years ago I co-wrote a book on racism in Canada, *Rivers Have Sources, Trees Have Roots.* We interviewed one hundred people—Native, Black, South-Asian and Chinese—about how racism affected their everyday life. In the book we talk about how the economic life of the country is racially stratified and how that stratification is held in place by a 'common-sense' racist ideology. It is within and through this common-sense racist ideology that cultural imperialism and appropriation take place. Assumptions of white racial superiority inform the designation of formal culture in this country and the assigning of public funds. Culture is organised around 'whiteness' through various 'para-statal' bodies, including the CBC, the NFB, the Canada Council, provincial and metropolitan arts councils, and through private media and cultural and educational institutions. Formal culture is itself stratified by class, gender and sexuality, organised around maleness, class and heterosexual privilege. In film, radio and television all one has to do is listen to the voices, watch the faces, note the choice of themes and point of view to get it. Simply, who is reflected there? This same 'commonsense' racist ideology questions the production of any cultural work by artists of colour and then dismisses or anoints it—and with far more dismissal than anointment. These works are 'placed' by their relationship to and relevance for the dominant cultural form. Reviewers always comment on the 'anger' in my work, for example, (anger having been categorised as a particularly 'Black' emotion) and on its portrayal of 'the Black experience'. White work, on the other hand, is never questioned for its portrayal of 'the white experience'. But this commonsense racist ideology is not one-dimensional or monolithic. You don't have to wear a sheet to take part in it. You don't even have to be white. You just have to absorb the taken-for-granted knowledge about race and racial difference produced through colonialism and Black slavery. This taken-for-granted knowledge is engaged in all the apparatus of 'sense making' in society: newspapers, educational institutions, visual and print text production, and in its reflection of the laissez-faire capitalism at its base it suggests supposed variations of opinion within the dominant political ideology. If you listened to the way debates are framed you would swear that these positions are radically different. In fact they are not. Liberal and conservative forces vie for power within the society, occupying and advocating various positions along a ruler of common-sense racist ideology where white supremacy is consistent. As long as formal Canadian culture looks like the National Ballet and the Toronto Symphony, white supremacy is operative. White skin is the signifier for socio-economic opportunity and privilege. 'Whiteness'—that set of essences and values claiming racial superiority—is the philosophical outgrowth of that opportunity and privilege. So European cultural forms (those appropriated by the white upper class at any rate)—the ballet, the European classical symphony, the European classical opera—are the signifiers for 'whiteness' as cultural superiority, cultural superiority, that is, that informs a notion of intellectual and evolutionary superiority and that legitimates white dominance as the logical outcome of Nature. Through these forms, groups of whites who have no role in structuring them buy into a notion of 'whiteness' as superior, even when their own lives are not mirrored there. Canadian national identity itself for many reasons is necessarily predicated on 'whiteness'. One key reason is the need to bolster an inferiority complex occasioned by Britain as its great intellectual mother and the United States as its rich bully cousin. What distinguishes Canada from other ex-colonies of Britain and other subordinates of the United States of America is its status as a 'white' nation. Brian Mulroney was always talking that white colonial talk about 'we in the civilised world', and then there are the perennial warnings in the daily press about Canada losing its 'English' and 'French' character to masses of 'immigrants'. These terms are euphemisms for white and Black, light and dark. The surfacing of the Heritage Front or the Aryan Nation recruiting young whites in Toronto high schools, swastika graffiti on synagogues and KKK cross burnings in southwestern Ontario—these are not anachronisms but the rabid voices of a pervasive ideology.

Canadian culture doesn't deal with the cultural work of all peoples of colour living here the same way, of course, and hence the different approaches to its imperialising effect. The material conditions of the groups, their history of struggle against oppression and the rhetorical tropes which they deploy in that struggle and in daily life, determined their strategies. While some Black strategy may take on access to publishing and reviewing, some First

Nations' strategy might take on the very act of saying. (The Black community's protest against the Royal Ontario Museum exhibit 'Into the Heart of Africa' and the exhibit's subsequent demise illustrate that these strategies are not mutually exclusive for any group of people.) There can be no question that Canadian culture has marauded the cultural production of the First Nations not to speak of their spiritual myths and icons and their land. White Canada's founding meaning was predicated on the conquest of First Nations' land, on the ossification of 'native spirituality' and mythos, and on the glorification of the conquering culture. The founding meaning is a new myth of origin which not only subordinates the 'native' culture but also legitimates the conquerors' ownership. This founding meaning must constantly prove its rightness and its superiority; the spoils of its conquests—the people and their culture—become artifacts of that conquest. So it is not in the least surprising that white writers would think that they had a 'right' to 'retell' or 'use' First Nations' stories, myths, etc. ... Whatever the reasons put forward for this using and retelling, the founding meaning lies at the core. And it is hardly surprising that First Nations people who contest this ownership say that no one but they should tell their stories, least of all those who benefit from the colonial conquest.

On the radio Neil Bissoondath says that he has

162

the right to write in the voice of a woman and in the voice of a Black person if he wants. Well, of course he has a 'right'—and 'right' may not be the correct word here at all—that is, he can. No one is stopping his hand, and those whom he rails against as wanting to stop him are certainly not in power in the publishing establishment of this country, so he need not fear them. However, it takes only an intelligent look to see that what people are saying is far more complex than he admits. There are far more numerous, diverse and incisive arguments on the side of the debate that says cultural appropriation is an issue than on the side that says it does not exist or that cultural work, literary work or the 'imagination' should be exempt from such criticism. Cultural appropriation is not an accusation, it is a critical category. It looks at the location of the text, and the author, in the world at specific historical moments: moments that give rise to gender-, race-, class-making, 'othering'; moments rooted in colonial conquest, in slavery and in economic exploitation. It investigates the positioning of the author within and apart from the text, and within the interaction of the text with colonial discourse, sexist discourse and racial discourse. It challenges the author's anonymity; it questions the author's 'interests' in the text; it argues that the author is not 'innocent' of the relations of race, gender, sexuality and class. And it locates the production of the text and the production of the author

164

within practices that give rise to gender, race, class subordination and colonial subjugation. It proposes that imagery, images, the imagination and represen-tation are deeply ideological in that they suggest ways of thinking about people and the world. This critique goes beyond the mere notion of 'good' and 'bad' representation; it is more concerned with how we see, enact and re-enact, make, define and rede-fine, vision how we lived and how we are going to live. So Neil Bissoondath may write in any voice he pleases. What I suggest however, is that we have a right to look at his texts through this critical analysis. We might want to say that his attempt to write in the voice of a young Japanese woman fails. His portray-al gives us no sense of her interior life, her own sense of her life, of her female body, given the particular set of historical, social, personal and emotional cir-cumstances under which she lived. Bissoondath only revalidates the myth of the 'Oriental' woman in Euro-centric discourse. He draws only the stereo-type so helpful in white domination. The authorial voice is intrusive and manipulative in the story, so it is difficult to gauge the character in terms of her agency or lack of it. The author never examines the Japanese in the white imagination or the woman in the male imagination with the care he ought to for his prose to lift itself above the normalised, racialised stereotype. And if I say that Bissoondath's young Black man in his story 'Guerrillas' only mimics

the well-worn American film stereotype and the
Hegelian representation of the 'clumsy', 'ignorant',
'primitive' African and that his story inscribes racial
inferiority as a feature of blackness and inscribes
blackness as intellectual inferiority and mocks the
great Civil Rights Movement of the sixties as inept
and misguided—if I say all this, which is not even all
that I could say of Bissoondath's woman voice and
his Black voice which are therefore not their voices at
all but his through the Euro-centric screen of racist,
sexist discourse—I might also say that he does himself no good here for these discourses seep into
places, into corners where he, too, lives in his
'racialised' self.

Which brings me to Neil Bissoondath's role in the
Canadian debate on cultural appropriation. It is
interesting that he has appeared quite often contesting the notion that voice can be appropriated. This is
noticeable precisely because he is a person of colour
and because those positing cultural appropriation as
a critique of Canadian literature are people of colour.
His testimony is more important than the testimony
of any white writer on the subject because supposedly we cannot claim that his opinions are textured
by his race alignment. We assume that he is cog-
nizant of colonial history, racism and so on, and so
does his audience, which makes his disagreement
supposedly all the more potent. And this is precisely his cachet for those on the other side of the debate

who are largely white and vested in the colonial representation of race. In producing a Neil Bissoondath to denounce the cultural appropriation critique, the white cultural establishment produces a dark face to dismiss and discredit all the other dark faces and simultaneously to confirm and reinscribe that colonial representation so essential to racial domination.

On a jury for the Governor General's Award for poetry, I fill two of the spaces for the 'marginalised'. I am a woman and I am Black. An immense amount of criticism, pressure and opposition from these communities over the last ten years has made my presence possible. My co-jurors are two middle-aged to older white men. We are clearly antithetical in terms of experience and opinion. In our initial selections, I differ more from them than they do from each other. I ask about the decision-making rules. The voice of the chair, strong with conviction or rectitude, tells me something nevertheless vague, like 'working our way through to consensus'. I say I'd like to vote, I'm fairly sure that there can be no consensus and I want my opposition registered. I do not want to be swept under these two white men's opinions and drowned in their 'Of course, Bill' and 'I agree with you there, Bob,' at the end of which the same old legitimating Euro-centric vision will emerge. I want to address blackness and 'whiteness', not gloss it over. The room becomes tense as I

explain that I want to state from the beginning that
we are unlikely to agree. Oh no, no, no, one of them
assures me, we already agree on some things and
I'm fascinated by your other choices, maybe we can
benefit from a lively discussion. I find this precious.
I insist that we have no basis for consensus, that we
acknowledge our differences—race, gender, class,
age, sexualities—and proceed, that we do not need
sameness for decision-making. One of them gets
benevolent and patronising, the other gets angry. I
take on my 'inclusion' on this jury and others, not as
a task of assimilation into Euro-centric values but as
contesting those very values and widening the sets
of cultural forms that come to stand for Canadian
culture. I bring to a jury another definition of the
meaning of poetry in everyday life. My tradition
says that your speech must be relevant, charged,
politically conscious, memorable. It must pursue
human freedom. Assimilation, however, is how
those in power translate oppositional claims, so my
co-jurors are probably piqued by my ingratitude. I
annoy everyone further by asking if a prize must be
given, the best book in any given year might not be
a good book at all. I ask, aren't we supposed to think
of our selections as a vision for a new Canadian
poetics? Well, of course, the day was horrendous and
I left with a headache that stretched to my toes
because ... no one wants to tell any one what to
write and we are only interested in the quality of the

work and quality is some kind of essence, impossible to pin down like the imagination, but identifiable, has nothing to do with what is said, but what is said should not be shrill.

'Culture,' Cabral says, 'is always in the life of a society (open or closed), the more or less conscious result of the economic and political activities of that society, the more or less dynamic expression of the kinds of relationships which prevail in that society ...'[16]

I only draw attention here to the dominant discourse on culture in Canada. Its response to criticism from people of colour, women, lesbians and gays and progressives has been to try to assimilate a few voices into the discourse without overturning it fundamentally. Yet more vibrant possibilities exist in the multitude of voices now emerging in this country. These voices see the imagination as transformative, as leading out of the pessimism of colonial discourse, as making new narratives ...

Seeing

The eye is a curious thing: it is not passive, not merely a piece of physiology, practical and utilitarian; it is not just a hunk of living matter, gristle, tendon, blood. It sees. It has more skill than the foot or hand. When it takes an image in, this act appears to me not simple. The eye has experience, knowledge and has cut out territories, reasons why it sees this subject leaning in and that one leaning away. Why does it see this face here and a hand moving across the plane of the face and shoulders there? The eye has citizenship and possessions. Else what makes me recognise Sherona's right hand at the beginning of the trajectory of her body reach across her face rapidly while her left plants itself on her left hip and her lips thin themselves on some precise word, the whole move describing her politics, her affirmation, her insistence and her don't-take-shit-from-nobody attitude? Yet this same body-statement makes my white cinematographer zoom in to her face only, filling the screen with it until all other gestures are absent. What makes this happen if the eye does not possess some frame through which seeing is composed? Frames perhaps already describing, perhaps not already as if born to it but born in it, already describing the edges of the picture and what must be at the focus. My frame sees her whole body as the sum of what she is saying. Without the hand leading the plane of her movement, without the hip, the arm akimbo, without this against her hips and her head shaking into it, she is not a won't-take-shit Black woman about to move out of your frame if you don't see me right and living not in this frame but doing it a favour standing here giving it this much time, don't buy this frame, this can never describe me, a full Black woman who's lived a life thoroughly devoted to messing up this bullshit. The white cinematographer's frame is somehow narrowed to Sherona's skin, the close-up searing about its texture, investigating its colour, giving it importance over her hands flying, her body steadying into her hip, her arm akimbo. In this frame her skin, instead, stretches like fabric across the frame and her mouth moving in it; the close-up comes tight, tight, trying to cut out the finger of the hand moving rapidly across the face, the mouth moving, it seems, with no sound, not interrupting the skin.

The eye has purpose and goes where it wants to in order to clarify itself. Or to repeat. It has fancies. Or to regulate. It is very precise as to how it wants to see the world. When I fully realise this two films later and do not leave the camera to the rules of the other eye, I receive a curious message from the head of camera. He does not like a certain shot; it is not a good shot, he says, and may be useless in the editing, it was obviously a mistake and why didn't we catch it, did I really want such a shot. In the shot Leleti is reading a poem to a woman out of the frame. She is angled off-camera left. You cannot see Leleti's eyes, but the woman the love poem is sent to can. I angle the shot this way and try to angle most of the film to include the possessing eyes, eyes which are beyond the eye that usually possesses. In this poem there are so many possessions beyond this one, so the body directly facing the camera would be capitulation to the eye that always possesses. The head of camera relays the message that he does not feel that the woman reading the lesbian poem is reading to him. No kidding, I relay to him. This is the eye that always looks and needs to be looked at.

You cannot leave this eye alone for a second, at least not if it's resting on you. It will fall back on itself, on things it knows.

Notes
for
Writing
thru
Race

I live in a culture where the dominant forces are still recapturing or repatriating what they perceive as their original cultural ideals, those of the motherland from which they were cast out or that they had to leave to make their fortunes. No matter the varied alignments, positions, the cultural elite in English Canada is constantly harking back to its origins as a source of its legitimation for its identity, for its nation-and state-building. Key to those origins is race, more specifically the characteristic of 'whiteness' as 'whiteness' situated itself in the identity, state-and nation-building of European colonisers. Built around the obvious and easy distinction of colour, 'whiteness' became more and more the way to differentiate the coloniser from the colonised. The European nation-state of Canada built itself around 'whiteness', differentiating itself through 'whiteness' and creating outsiders to the state, no matter their claims of birthright or other entitlement. Inclusion in or access to Canadian identity, nationality and citizenship (de facto) depended and depends on one's relationship to this 'whiteness.' While it is not the only characteristic it is the dominant characteristic. It has a certain elasticity. One can enter not only if one belongs to the so-called founding nations—the English and the French—but also other European nationalities like the German or Ukrainian. Its flexibility and its strength allow it to contain inter-ethnic squabbles, like that between the English and the French, without rending its basic fabric of white entitlement. The way in which that squabble dominates and preoccupies the political life of the country, regardless of, say, indigenous peoples' claims to the land reveals the predominance of white entitlement. The elasticity of 'whiteness' can also swallow Ukrainians, Germans, Scottish newcomers and within a generation cleanse Italians, Portuguese, Eastern Europeans, etc. which is why we often read in the newspapers comments and letters, largely from these co-opted groups, decrying 'people who come to Canada should just become Canadians' or 'When I came to this country there was no multiculturalism, you could not expect a grant or anything, you just had to fit in.' Well, of course, the truth is that when they came to this country they slipped into 'whiteness' which the Canadian state-legitimating process had assigned as its main characteristic and which coincided with their race. Consider the differential treatment of people other than whites in immigration policy over the last century. And of course they got a grant—'whiteness'. It was like money and still is. That is why when, according to Bronwyn Drainie in the *Globe and Mail*, Robert Fulford, the doyen of Canadian culture, says that colour is his least important feature, he is, of course, disingenuous. He could not exist without it. It is responsible for his entry and location in the myth-making intellectual elite of the nation-state and for his role in the debate on racism in the arts. His role as defender of Canadian (read 'white') culture is understandable—and crucial— precisely within this context. He is doing the most important part of his job as a member of the white cultural elite by using all the discursive strategy— implying that race does not exist, emptying 'skin colour' of its acknowledged political meanings, invoking liberalism, appealing to rights won through Black struggle as if he had a role in their accomplishment, paternalistically warning those whom racism affects most that they are going down the wrong path in how they choose to organise against it, positioning himself as objective and omniscient observer with no politico-racial interest—and means—the *Globe and Mail*, the organ of the neo-conservative, corporate capital elite—which has grown more rabidly conservative, if that is at all possible, since the defeat of the Conservative Party in the last Canadian elections—to attack outsiders, to defend the elite and the organising characteristic of the nation-state. Fulford's attack indicates the depth of the ideological-cultural struggle facing 'whiteness' in Canada—the face-off between 'whiteness' and all it has excluded. But 'excluded' is too benign a word for the denial of history and must now be used carefully as must all words which begin as oppositional tools and become co-opted by state institutions and the white cultural establishment. Perhaps we should talk again about the repression of our cultures by this concept of 'whiteness'. We haven't been excluded, we've been repressed, and we don't need access, we need freedom from the tyranny of 'whiteness' expressing itself all through our lives.

Access, representation, inclusion, exclusion, equity. All are other ways of saying race in this country without saying that we live in a deeply racialised and racist culture which represses the life possibilities of people of colour. We have to be careful of the way those words have become bureaucratic glosses for human suffering. We have to notice how those words deceptively explain away the vulgar, privileging, power relations that whites in the country don't want to admit to or give up. It is possibly a very Canadian strategy to create these glosses—just as royal commissions and committees to study problems are particularly Canadian—to delay and put a distance between the problem and the answer. Giving up power, sharing the cultural, political and economic space and eschewing the whole apparatus for which 'whiteness' is useful, is really the solution. If Robert Fulford had come to terms with or admitted any of this, he might have, blushing, held his peace. Instead, quite amazingly, we have the spectre of all the big white men (Michel Dupuis, Richard Gwyn, Robert Fulford) in Canada, representatives and spokesmen for the power elites, suddenly talking about 'skin colour', warning us coloureds that we view it too simplistically, warning that we're practising racism by mentioning it and organising around it. Quite curious all the big white men defining racism to the people who suffer it, chatting away to themselves and each other about how misguided we are. What deep racial scar do they speak from, what bitter knowledge? Now all the big white men are speaking in unison—the ones who speak on art and culture, the ones who speak on politics, even the ones who speak on foreign policy.

In truth, they are all responding to a general panic running through white Canadian society about the presence and claims of people of colour and the self-destructive outcomes of years of enduring racism. That this presence has finally drawn the attention of the cultural elite, which dismissed, ignored, discriminated against and did not notice that we were not in rooms when they were meeting, and didn't call it exclusion or apartheid when their gatherings were lily-white, that we have drawn their attention speaks to the depth of the panic. How else would we explain the white frenzy over a conference of First Nations and writers of colour—the almost weekly diatribes, the editorial vitriol, the white rage, the leaps in logic, the *obsession* for god's sake of white commentators?

178

I still get asked in interviews, 'Is there racism in this country?' Unlike the United States, where there is at least an admission of the fact that racism exists and has a history, in this country one is faced with a stupefying innocence. We have a deeper problem. It is this 'innocence' that causes people of colour to modify their claims to words such as 'access', 'representation' and 'inclusion' instead of entitlement. Here we get caught in the trap of numbers, percentages, as if the percentage of justice in the society should match the percentage of people of colour in the population. How much is that? Twenty percent. Each demand for an end to racism is met with reductionism and subject to the most limited revisionist application. What we are debating in the end is what a society sees, must find, as important to its psychic, moral and human self. What we are debating in the end is whether this country intends to give people of colour full human rights as opposed to provisional human rights, whether it is willing to shed the sophistry of its 'innocence'.

As I said earlier, we live in a culture where the dominant forces are still recapturing or repatriating what they perceive as their original cultural ideals. That makes a culture static since it is not interested in carrying on, moving ahead, but in rescuing what it did not have or did not feel entitled to back home. So its sense of those ideals is romantic, nostalgic, superficial. The English Canada that I live in is always surprised by and resistant to cultural interventions from people it does not recognise as fitting into its imposed norms. Caribana, even though it draws the largest number of tourists to Canada, fights in racially hostile territory every year for viability and acceptance. Sikhs, even though they fought in the Second World War, cannot walk into a Legion Hall while wearing a turban. Jewish people, even though they died in that war, encounter the same xenophobia. The rumblings from its own centre are themselves quickly marginalised or co-opted; Rick Salutin writes for the *Globe*, for example.

Once I went to the Notting Hill Gate Carnival in London. Arriving at Ladbrooke Grove, I was struck by a strange feeling of time warp. The mas costumes had a sense of stasis. They felt like, looked like, they were being worn in the fifties. Then I realised that the people who had made them had left Trinidad in the fifties, and it must have been that they carried their sense of Carnival as it was then with them, preserving it intact, never moving on because they needed to hold on to it as it was to survive the new country. Or they needed to bring it as they felt it then. This culture has a similar sense of warp, except that it is not an oppressed culture and can impose this warp on all it considers outsiders. It imposes this stasis on all discussion also, so we have the situation where in 1994 its artists and social commentators refuse to admit the existence of an ideology some five hundred or more years old through which their ancestors arrived and prospered in this part of the world and through which they continue to benefit. But of course it is more than warp; it is living and has great impact on our daily life, and though the culture may ease eager agreement out of white immigrants for the notion of Anglo culture, we are unwilling and unable to be filled by this, just as we are unable inevitably to qualify for the grant of 'whiteness'.

On
Poetry

Every word turns on itself, every word falls after it is said. None of the answers that I've given over the years is the truth. Those answers have all been given like a guerrilla with her face in a handkerchief, her eyes still. She is still, poised for quick movement, but still. Her boots sturdy, the gravel under them dislodges and dusts. But her eyes are still. And I've answered like the captive giving answers in an interrogation, telling just enough to appease the interrogator and just enough to trace the story so she could repeat it without giving anything away and without contradiction the next time she has to tell it. I've told them the same things over and over again, and I'll tell them again when they ask because they only ask certain questions, like where I'm from and do I hate them.

But if I can give myself a moment, I would say it's

been relief to write poetry, it's been just room to live.

I've had moments when the life of my people has been so overwhelming to bear that poetry seemed useless, and I cannot say that there is any moment that I do not think that now. At times it has been more crucial to wield a scythe over high grass in a field in Marigot; at times it has been more important to figure out how a woman without papers in Toronto can have a baby and not be caught and deported; at times it has been more helpful to organise a demonstration in front of the police station at Bay and College Streets. Often there's been no reason whatsoever to write poetry. There are days when I cannot think of a single reason to write this life down.

There's a photograph of me when I was four. I'm standing next to my little sister and my cousin. My big sister is in the picture, too. I do not resemble myself except for my legs, which were bowed and still are. My little sister is crying, her fingers in her mouth, and my cousin looks stunned, as if she's been thrown into the picture. My big sister is tall and slender, heading for the glamour which will describe her life. She looks like Nancy Wilson. Black patent-leather shoes, white boat-necked dress. I am looking at the camera, my mouth open. I am holding a shac-shac, blurring in the picture, so that my little sister would stop crying. I look as if I'm trying to make this picture work. I remember the moment of consciously getting set, holding the shac-shac, being called upon to act, saying to my little sister don't cry, see, don't cry. My eyes in the picture are not those of a little girl; they seem knowledgeable, still. My little sister's eyes look teary, my cousin's, frightened, my big sister's, sad. Mine, still. Watching. I remember watching. Knowing that this was an occasion to watch out of ourselves and saying I'd hold the shac-shac so my little sister would not cry. I only recognise my legs and the eyes. Still. Watching out.

183

If I can take a second. Shaking the gravel from my shoes. Poetry is here, just *here*. Something wrestling with how we live, something dangerous, something honest.

Notes

1 Janice Lee Liddell, 'The Narrow Enclosure of Motherdom/Martyrdom ...' in *Out of the Kumbla*, Carol Boyce Davies and Elaine Fido, eds., p. 321.

2 Earl Lovelace, *The Wine of Astonishment*, p. 44.

3 Merle Hodge, *Crick Crack Monkey*, p. 16.

4 Ibid., pp. 18-19.

5 Joan Riley, *The Unbelonging*, p. 9.

6 Ibid., p. 143.

7 Ibid., p. 45.

8 Ibid., p. 52.

9 Jamaica Kincaid, *At the Bottom of the River*, p. 55.

10 Ibid., p. 58.

11 James Baldwin, *The Fire Next Time*, pp. 34-35.

12 Ibid., p. 31.

13 Ibid., pp. 32-33.

14 Ibid., p. 30.

15 Amilcar Cabral, *Return to the Source*. Monthly Review Press, NY, 1973, p. 39.

16 Ibid., p. 41.

Acknowledgements

'Notes for Writing thru Race' was delivered at the Writing
Thru Race conference, Vancouver, June 1994.
'Whose Gaze and Who Speaks for Whom' appeared in *Brick*,
Summer 1993.
'Bread out of Stone' appeared in *Language in Her Eye*, Coach
House Press, 1990.
'Just Rain, Bacolet' appeared in *Writing Away*, McClelland &
Stewart, 1994.

Thanks to Patricia Murphy. Thanks also to Faith Nolan,
Filomina Carvalho and Leleti Tamu for reading and
listening to the work.

About the Author

Dionne Brand was born in 1953 in Guayguayare, Trinidad. In 1970, she moved to Toronto, and in 1975 she graduated from the University of Toronto with a degree in English and Philosophy. She received an MA in History and Philosophy from the Ontario Institute for Studies in Education in 1989.

Since coming to Canada, Brand has participated in many ways in the Black and feminist communities. She has worked on behalf of youth, education, immigrant women, trade unions and battered women. Out of these experiences came the volume *Rivers Have Sources, Trees Have Roots: Speaking of Racism*, 1986 (with K. Sri Bhaggiyadatta), and *No Burden To Carry: Narratives of Black Working Women in Ontario*, 1991.

Dionne Brand has also published six books of poetry, most recently *No Language Is Neutral*, and a book of short stories, *Sans Souci and Other Stories*. She has been writer-in-residence at the University of Toronto and has taught at the University of Guelph.

Brand also works in documentary film. She was the associate director and writer of *Older, Stronger, Wiser*, a portrait film about older Black women in Canada, and she was the co-director of *Sisters in the Struggle*, a documentary about contemporary Black women activists in Canada. *Long Time Comin'*, her latest film, looks at the art and politics of singer-musician Faith Nolan and painter Grace Channer.